"Nominated several times for the Nobel Prize for Literature, winner of a number of international literary prizes, and translated into over twenty languages, Gennady Aygi is regarded as one of the most important Russian poets of the second half of the 20th century. He is a poet of the country and stands totally against the classical tradition of Russian poetry from Pushkin to Brodsky."  —*Poetry London Newsletter*

"In the poetry of Gennady Aygi, the fragmented typography and distrust of Meaning and Reference that we associate with modernity interact with the pagan dances and songs of the poet's ancient ancestral culture to produce a poetry at once familiar, unfamiliar, and distinctly Aygi's own."  —*American Book Review*

"Aygi writes with an imagistic compression and real time candor that is utterly unique."  —*Publishers Weekly*

"There is a recurring and compelling quality of *wonder* in Aygi's poetry. . . . He is a genius of liminal or border states—of perceptions that are altering, moments in our own processes of formation marked by a momentary slippage."  —*Rain Taxi*

"Gennady Aygi is a major and original voice in contemporary poetry."  —*Journal of European Studies*

"As a reader from the democratic West, it almost hurts to read the work of a man so intoxicated with wonder. But Gennady's poems are more than paeans: they are venerations to the non-rational and non-material . . . Within these breathless exclamations he echoes Emily Dickinson or-Wordsworth."  —Mary Gladstone, *The Scotsman*

"The most original voice in contemporary Russian poetry, and one of the most unusual voices in the world."  —Jacques Roubaud, *Times Literary Supplement*

# FIELD -
# RUSSIA

## ПОЛЕ-РОССИЯ

ПОЛЕ–РОССИЯ

С. Б.

вот и желаю тебе!

/счастье-молитва безмолвно/

в поле умолкнуть душою /"о Бог" говорим мы

более–сердцем: долиной

белым-блистающего

вольно

вокруг

Совершенства/ о как этот ветер

даже сиянье не тронул дыханья!

огнь

неизменности

веял

заметное

все

исчезало: о будь же

там

уже очень давно

не знающим – кем улыбалось:

"лучшее Чистое – ты"

1980

The poem "Field-Russia" in a letter by Gennady Aygi to Peter France

# GENNADY AYGI

# FIELD-
# RUSSIA

*translated from the Russian by* PETER FRANCE

A NEW DIRECTIONS PAPERBOOK ORIGINAL

ACKNOWLEDGMENTS

Poems in this volume have appeared (sometimes in earlier versions) in the following publications: "Willows," "Field-Russia, "In the Mist," "Again – Willows," "And – Schubert," "Rose of Silence," "The Last Ravine," "Leaf-fall and Silence," and "Final Departure" in *Gennady Aygi: Selected Poems 1954-94*, Angel Books, London / Hydra Books (Northwestern University Press), Evanston, Illinois (1997). "Final Departure" in *Index on Censorship*, London (1993). "Field: and Beyond it a Ruined Church," "View with Trees," and "Little Song about a Loss" in *Degree: of Stability*, Duration Press, Sausalito, CA (1999).

The poems have been translated from Aygi's typescripts, taking account of corrections made by him in subsequent Russian publications, in particular *Zdes'* (Moscow: Sovremennik, 1991); *Teper' vsegda snega* (Moscow: Sovetskii Pisatel', 1992); and *Poslednii Ot'ezd* (Moscow: OGI, 2001). The Russian text of "Conversation at a Distance" is published in *Razgovor na rasstoyanii* (St. Petersburg: Nimbus Press, 2001).

Manufactured in the United States of America
New Directions Books are printed on acid-free paper
First published as a New Directions Paperbook (NDP1085) in 2007
Published simultaneously in Canada by Penguin Books Canada Limited

Library of Congress Cataloging-in-Publication Data

Aygi, Gennady, 1934–2006.
[Poems. English. Selections]
Field-Russia / Gennady Aygi; translated from the Russian by Peter France.
    p. cm.
"A New Directions Paperbook Original."
ISBN 978-0-8112-1721-7 (pbk.: alk. paper)
1. Aygi, Gennady, 1934–2006—Translations into English.
I. France, Peter, 1935–   II. Title
PG3478.135A2 2007
891.71'44—dc22                                        2007025079

New Directions Books are published for James Laughlin
by New Directions Publishing Corporation
80 Eighth Avenue, New York, NY 10011

*And – it seems that Silence itself,*
*entering a pile of papers,*
*Itself crosses out thoughts about Itself,*
*striving – fusing with me –*
*to become:*
*Unique*
*and ever more –*
*Absolute*

GENNADY AYGI
from *Poetry-as-Silence,* 1992

This translation is dedicated to the memory of Gennady Aygi,
dear friend and enduring presence.

# Contents

# FIELD - RUSSIA

*ПОЛЕ-РОССИЯ*

# CONVERSATION AT A DISTANCE

## (ANSWERS TO A FRIEND'S QUESTIONS)

Note: *This text was first published in a Yugoslav literary newspaper on September 25, 1985. The questions were asked by the poet Nikola Vujčić; the answers were given in writing.*

*Could you say something about the blurring of the frontier between waking and sleep in your poetry?*

As far as I can remember – for more than a quarter of a century now – almost all the poetry surrounding me has been direct, "committed" poetry, very often of a rather basic kind. It was always the poetry of action, of "acts." I could sense no poetic truth, no "real" or living truth, in the way these "acts" were directed.

Consequently, if I was to find poetic truth, the truth of human existence (or to put it more exactly, of human *endurance of life*), I had to look within myself, in my memory and my way of seeing and understanding the world. I did not need to engage in "acts," whether they were "poetic" or "real-life" (and indeed, as I saw it, such acts were not needed by anyone else; – there were others who "acted" in poetry more skilfully than I could).

I gradually began to set something different against the poetry of "acts." It was not exactly contemplation. No, it was something else, an ever increasing immersion in a kind of *self-preserving unity* of what I can best describe as something "undiminishing-abiding," something from which human intervention had not yet brought forth the phenomenon known as an "act."

It seems to me that the theme of *sleep* gradually and imperceptibly emerged from this "literary situation" of mine. Sleep-as-phenomenon, but also sleep-as-atmosphere became for me the *sleep-image* of a certain world, a sleep-world in which one could reach out toward "islands," toward fragments of a "river-bed" that constituted the life-endurance of a person; – there was the feeling that in pain and with pain – in a kind of fire-focus – I was touching the changing manifestations of the being in the world of a single existence-fate.

In this situation I made great use of *sleep* itself as an image. The refusal of "action" naturally also took the form of *silence*, and *quietness* became the symbol of the ongoing endurance of life. In short, there was one single sleep-world, which encompassed both sleep and waking. In such cases, it is obviously difficult to draw a line between waking and sleep. I only know that "waking" sometimes comes into my poetry when I "get out of myself," and in art this seems to me a bad, destructive sign (just as in life it is better not to get "beside yourself" with rage).

*What of the poetic text as a "body," a sign on the paper?*

The verbal "text" as a body . . . In the first place, I see it perhaps not on paper, but in some created "paperless" space.

Even any coherent oral text is a "body" . . . – it resembles a bush, stretching skyward. There are some unforgettable text-"bodies" of this kind. For instance, I feel the liturgy to be a kind of "spiritual body" in the church – it is "constructively" organized, possessing its own church-like shape, and its outlines imprint themselves on the mind and the memory.

Ideally, I feel the poetic text to be a "body" of this sort. As against the classic European verse forms (quatrains, octaves, sonnets, etc.), every poem in free verse makes its appearance (I am thinking here of its external appearance) as a kind of unrepeatable temple, a kind of verbal-spiritual structure, visible in its verbal outlines, unlike any other "canonic" structure. Because of its inner unity of construction (the whole thing is "of a piece"), such a work calls for an indivisible coherence of all its graphic constituents. However this may be, I give quite serious consideration to such matters. I think this concern for

4

the "body" of the thing on paper also reflects my "popular" rural origins. For instance, all my poems have a title (if a title is missing, I simply call the poem "untitled"), as if I could not bear to see any "constructions" – even verbal ones – that lack a "roof." The same applies to the dating of every poem: I see the date as playing a "constructive" part in the unified "building" of the work.

For the most part I hear poems "liturgically," and perhaps I see them this way too – when they are not yet built on the paper and rising above it. The liturgy combines the chant, the Word-Logos, and the "intonation of the soul" – almost like a wordless conversation! – and it contains both invisible ("spiritual") and visible ("ritual") signs. It seems then that I conceive "the poetic text as a body and a sign on paper" in this way: as the generic form of some kind of verbal "temple," which, being itself a kind of generic sign, manifests itself in more "concrete" inner signs of what it contains – when I want these to be particularly visible, I pick them out in italic or *razriadka* (the addition of extra space between letters), sometimes introducing hieroglyphs and ideograms, and deliberately highlighted "white places" (also signs, each with its own special "meaning").

There are times when a separate poem of mine (usually a short one) is a complete sign in itself (that is to say, the "body" of the text compressed into a single sign). But only a few of my poems are like this.

*What is the origin of the themes of sleep, field, and forest in your poetry?*

I have already said quite a lot about the theme of sleep in my poems. I would just add that *action* as a concept and as a phenomenon always conceals a trap – aiming for one thing, we may arrive at something quite different. I do not fear the trap of *sleep*, since it is more an education of the "soul" than a temptation for it.

As for my other themes – *field and forest* ... – I was born and grew up in a Chuvash village, surrounded by boundless forests, the windows of our house looked out directly over the fields – field and forest made up "my whole world." Through world literature I became acquainted with the "ocean-worlds" and "city-worlds" of other peoples, and I attempted to give to my "Forest-Field" world as much meaning as other well-known "worlds." I even wanted it to possess – as far as possible – some kind of "universal meaning" (drawing on the whole of my intellect and imagination, which had been educated by other cultures in a long, strenuous process – my comparative-cultural "baggage" had to be as extensive and elaborate as possible, becoming "my own," always ready to be called on and to be "set to work" in my creative activity, without any limits whatsoever).

I wanted the "small" to be elevated to the Great, I wanted to give it universal significance. And in fact this has always been the case in various literatures and cultures. The concept of the "provincial" cannot be applied to fields and haystacks – there is nothing *provincial* about the earth. The haystacks and fields of Normandy became universal once the Impressionists had touched them.

In short the *fields* and *forests* in my poems are simply *faces* of my motherland, which have undoubtedly become more and more symbolic in character.

There can be very simple desires in art – for instance the simple desire to tell other people – people of different landscapes and cultures – about the appearance of one's own country. This was the origin of "my" *fields* and *forests*, and equally of my *snow*, whose whiteness grew "into a symbol."

The Italian literary scholar Giovanna Pagani-Cesa has written a substantial study of "archetypes" in my poetry, showing deep links between such key images as "field," "forest," "white" (various degrees of white), "snow" or "window" and important elements in ancient Chuvash pagan mythology. I agree with Giovanna "on all points," though I have to say that naturally I was not thinking about any "archetypes" when I wrote my poems.

*What are your thoughts about poetry and tradition?*

It seems to me that the problems of "tradition" and "traditions" are of more concern to scholars and critics than to poets and writers (what is more, critics generally engage in this debate with a certain "conservationist" ardor). They speak about traditions as if they were telling us: "be like this or that writer," prompting us to write in the manner of one writer or to "build images" according to the method of another. They make exceptions in favor of the "successors"; as you learn from the classics, you can still bring "something" of your own to literature (always with the approval of the critics, of course). But I can take account of "traditions," Pushkin for instance, precisely by not following them, overcoming them in the name of my own poetic vision (and in doing so, I am the only one who knows in what ways and for what I can be grateful to Pushkin).

My own literary education can be traced to something different. In the most difficult periods of my life, my thoughts turned frequently and intensively to Nietzsche and Baudelaire, and more recently to Cyprian Kamil Norwid; it was as if I was addressing the writers themselves rather than their ideas, whether literary or otherwise. For instance, the spiritual-intellectual *image* of Baudelaire as an existential martyr, Baudelaire-as-Image, was more important for me than any "traditions" (including his own literary traditions). Like Blok, he aided me in my own self-education as a "poet" (I am sure that every poet must go through a very difficult period of "artistic" self-education). You could say that I tried to learn from Baudelaire both fidelity to Poetry (as he and I understood it) and the way a poet should lead his life (in this domain I made some serious mistakes).

In this way, the continuingly influential and genuinely *living images* of certain teachers constituted for me their "legacy," their lifelong support, and the strength of this kind of "contact" was more powerful than any literary considerations.

*What linguistic operations are needed for the poet to "command" language?*

I am reminded of the dictum of Apollinaire: "You can paint a picture with dung, or with a pipe, just so long as it is a picture."

As I see it, all means are suitable for attaining a "command" of language. The most outlandish "wild" creation, if it is *genuine*, inevitably possesses its own inner harmony, any "unacceptable" element in it will "have its place," will be "canonic," since every successful work is in itself "canonic." (A still more important "canon" is the inevitability of this creative law – breaking out of one circle, we find ourselves in another, stronger circle.)

Similarly, there are no linguistic means that are laid down once and for all. Some twenty years ago I worked on *syntax* – in a way I was trying to relate it to the changes that had taken place in people's ways of relating to one another (sentences left unfinished, things left unsaid, absence of "explanatory" words, "password"-words, pauses that expressed what is behind the "word sequence" – a kind of sorrowful and indeed hopeless commentary, as if I were saying: "but who will hear this").

Now things are rather different . . . – my wish is to *say as little as possible*, aiming in this way to allow non-human quietness and light to grow ever greater and "more irreversible" all around. How does this work in cases that seem to be more or less successful? I note one thing: that something that is waveringly alogical, something previously unknown, becomes fully logical thanks to this work, as if I was learning to talk in a language that was new to me.

*What of the energy of language and the poet?*

The sea and the wind are powerful in themselves – "even without us." Language is the same. The poet *enters* language and language "goes to work" in accordance with his energy. But be careful . . . – they are not fully "identical." Be careful . . . – even in a weakened state you perceive such crests and valleys of language: its own "autonomous" energy seems to be seething there, taking on "a life of its own," and you may manage to channel some of this energy "to your own account" into your already cooling poetry – even in an enfeebled state you have *glimpsed* something, and this too is work: the force that did not submit to strength may submit to your tact, your intuition, your skill.

*Thinking of the technique of verse – what should a poem be today?*

In my view of things there is no such thing as technique waiting to be "deployed." "Technique" comes into being in the "fire" and "body" of writing itself. I feel the poem of today to be "free," that is to say that it can absorb any kind of rhythm and "meter," not shunning even rhyme, but easily able to do without it . . . – a poem of this kind is as it were like *nature*: it is the free field and forest, not a "classical park." The champions of aristocratic "order," some of whom exist even today, ought to take their thinking a little further, they ought to envisage some further development: in the last analysis nothing is free in artistic creation (and this unfreedom is the one universal and obligatory Canon): "free verse" has its own measures and proportions, its "classicism" finds its place one way or another in the unbroken circle of the Meta-Classical – it surrounds us, like some distant, *ultimate* hoop.

Possibly one can see in "free verse" signs that we are unconsciously trying to get away from the centuries-old, sclerotic city culture; – the capacious, multifaceted free poem, with its "non-unified" forms of expressiveness and its intermittent alternation of various levels of content is perhaps akin to a distinctive "model of nature."

*What have you to say about poetry and shamanism?*

This theme (or problem) has an artificial look to it. If we perceive a sort of magic-making in the songs of a contemporary Chukot poet, we accept it without misgivings. But "shamanistic" or "Zen-Buddhist" elements cannot simply be assimilated in order to give new life to sophisticated European poetry; it is not possible to enrich life-giving or life-enhancing poetry with this kind of "learning." Our knowledge of others should send us back to ourselves.

If shamanistic shuddering-shouting awakens something real in the depths of our native poetic sound, the poet must expect to undertake a most painful descent into the forgotten deep places of the Melos-Fatherland – one must hear oneself, oneself alone. It is good if an interest in shamanism results for the poet in such *genuine* self-revelation.

*Poetry and experimentation?*

I have never *experimented* – I simply have no time for it.

Writings of mine which have an "experimental" look to them were always for me the only possible means and form of expression, once I had got rid of the old methods and forms that went with the theme in question. On such occasions it was as if I "exploded" in some new and unexpected fashion – exploded from the impossibility of using a language that seemed to me too old to express something that I had conceived.

I respect experimental poets (perhaps as martyrs of a paradoxical spirit). I follow their experiments with interest. At the same time, I do not know whether their researches and their discoveries in the way of "naturally-free" poetry are necessary, or whether they are more interesting to linguists. The new in poetry, as I see it, comes into being organically – thanks to a general linguistic incandescence, and not through "experiments."

*Poetry and quietness?*

Even "objective" quietness begins to exist for us only when we hear it, that is when we begin to converse with it.

The Noise-World sometimes begins to seem like a Lie-World – who can "purify" it to the point of *quietness*? – perhaps only art. One has to do more than simply "converse with quietness." In poetry it seems that one also must be able to *create quietness*.

And this is the paradox: In poetry, alongside speaking, there is also silence, but it too can only be created through the Word: the poetry of silence speaks, but in a different way . . . – how this works for me, or for any other poet (if indeed it does work) is the business of those who study literature, of the *philosophy of literature* (I think there is a philosophy of literature just as there is a philosophy of history).

But let us return to "objective" quietness. This is not the *Taoist nothingness*; created and creatable quietness is already a kind of Word that is brought into the world, and this Word can come into poetry, too. When and how? We don't know, or if we do, it is like a blind person imagining a kind of "seeing," which is known to him only through the words of others. But even so we must believe that it is not merely the reflection of meaning-quietness, but quietness *itself* that can imperceptibly find its place in poetry, when without suspecting it we receive the gift of enchantment . . . – "the world does not transcend us, we are the world" – the *shining* of that *single-abiding* can touch our paper . . . – just now I said that one must be able to "create quietness," but that is not quite correct, – in the noise of the world-as-action, one must set aside some time for "serving quietness," and then ways of expressing it will appear, differently for each poet.

In the 1960s I went through a brief period that I think of as my "Webern period." *Quietness* entered my poems in the shape of substantial semantic pauses which might last as long as a given verbally-sonorous "period of time." Now I aim more and more for a single unified poem that will represent in some way *quietness* "itself" . . . – as I have just said, this is only possible by means of words, and I can quite imagine that these attempts of mine may leave "scars" of despair in the poems rather than even a few "influxes" of *quietness*.

Sometimes "working theories" may arise in our minds for a short time (subsequently disappearing or being transformed). Once I developed the idea that music is the superseding of audibility by the Audible, and painting the superseding of visibility by the Visible. What then was poetry? Perhaps the superseding of the practical "communicative" word by the essential Word in which lies hidden the quietness of the pre-Word (one can say that the *essence* of the human being in the world is the *word in him or her*, or even more accurately, that in the world there is the *human-being-as-Word*).

*How do you see free verse in contemporary Russian poetry?*

As I see it, free verse remains completely undeveloped in contemporary Russian poetry. The free verse you come across is essentially *narrative* or *storytelling* (like a sort of prose with traces of a kind of "poetic" adornment – which looks extremely feeble). Or there is another type of free verse that crops up now and again – the *intellectual-rhetorical*.

I have observed that free verse (in any language, I think) is subject to one main danger: the *element of musicality*, which is inherent in poetry, is liable to dwindle – to the point of completely disappearing.

"Classical verse" in contemporary Russian poetry is undoubtedly undergoing an unprecedented crisis. In the post-war period, as if "for the last time," it was still living, thanks only to the inner semantic significance of the work of Pasternak, Akhmatova, and Zabolotsky. In reading it we trusted the *intonations of the great writers* – it was only these *intonations*, which could be distinguished thanks to the greatness of the individuals who revealed themselves in them, that still gave life to this old form of verse. The intonations of mediocre poets are hardly distinguishable from one another, and poems in "classical form" now resemble one and the same *little song* (even a music-hall song, if one is to be honest).

*Ideally*, "free verse," thanks to its "unmetrified" and genuinely free

rhythm, and thanks to its freedom from "stanzaism" (which is re-
placed by *periods* of verbal sonority of different lengths, not divided
up in an unchanging, standard manner, and by pauses of different
"magnitude"), such "free verse," I repeat, could, in contrast to the
above-mentioned monotonous unvarying "little song," find antece-
dents in various kinds of instrumental chamber music – so important
does it seem to me to preserve the *element of musicality* in so-called
*vers libre.*

*How does your poetry relate to symbolism and futurism?*

Thomas Mann called Rilke a great lyric poet, but noted at the same
time that there is "a lot of masculine muck" in his poems.

In symbolism there is a lot of "religious muck" which is found in
"symbols" that are not tested against genuine religious experience.

One might well not wish to confront symbolism with this "reck-
oning," since poetry is not something that is simply applied to
religion – poetry remains poetry, its essential goal being the develop-
ment of its own poetic means.

In this respect, symbolism must be considered as an *impressionism*
of the Word. All poetry up to symbolism-impressionism seems like a
single classical whole, a classicism with its different periods (both the
language of the Renaissance and the language of Goethe are an objec-
tivized language – the personality, even when it reveals its own peculi-
arities, can only express itself through this objectivized language – it is
sometimes sad to hear Beethoven, for instance, bursting his way
through this language – bursting out and then, as if suddenly realizing
what he has done, immediately "taking himself in hand").

From the point of view of language, impressionism (in which I in-
clude symbolism in poetry) seems to me the last great period in the
universal history of art. *The manifestation of subjectivity* and *subjective
language* became "legitimate" and generally accepted. It seems to me

that since that time nothing "fundamentally-new" has happened, that we still find ourselves in the continuing stream, the sphere and the world of impressionism. Dadaism, surrealism, and futurism can all be seen as simply variations prolonging the great "impressionist era" in art.

Russian poetic symbolism gave the word a richness of nuance, a multifaceted radiation, and abolished the familiar "one-dimensional" nature of the previous poetic word. I think this is the source of my indebtedness to Russian symbolism, and above all to Blok.

In futurism (as was the case with "symbols" in symbolism) it was precisely its "futurologies" that were revealed to be social utopias untested against any experience (worse still, the favorite images and ideas of the futurists turned out to be monstrosities). The "positive" element here is again concerned with the achievements of futurism in relation to the Word, which for the futurists came to be seen as palpably material – words began to have a differential "weight" that could be skillfully altered, it became possible to increase, diminish, and variously modify the "magnitude" of any individual word.

I have spoken more than once about the relation of my poetic work to Russian futurism. In doing so, I have always stressed, as I do now, that there is a certain period in my writing that I regard as influenced by Malevich rather than clearly allied to futurism (I think the "essence" of the ideas and content of my work is largely directed precisely *against* the programmatic and ideological essence of futurism; in relation to language, however, I learned a lot from the poetics of the Russian literary avant-garde that we are discussing).

Now indeed is the time – as I see it – to speak of what might be called the *spiritual* essence of both symbolism and futurism. It is time to state firmly that this essence turned out to be *untested* against the experience which – like it or not – must be unambiguously called *Christian-religious* (other "truths," in my view, have in great measure shown themselves to be real pseudo-spiritual traps from which there is no escape).

*Childhood and poetry – what can you say about the relationship between them?*

Perhaps in contemporary poetry we need to approach childhood-as-phenomenon not only in terms of "heart-and-feeling," but also as a matter of principle. It's not just a question of our need for that re-membered "freshness of impressions." In childhood we trusted the world more – it stood open to us, and was for us a veritable world-Universum.

We should do well to remember this. For in our *perception of the world* (not our knowledge) we have shrunk the world-as-universe to an incredible degree, turning it into a little bazaar-world – no wider than "orbits around the Earth." Isn't it true that precisely in this "cos-mic age" we have less and less feeling for *universality*, for the World-as-Universum? This little world of earthly fear and fears . . . – do we really experience anything beyond this?

So let us not be condescending to the phenomenon-of-childhood, enraptured as it is by the miracle of the existence of the inexplicably-meaningful world (much in nature itself shows that it was not created for man alone).

The "theme of childhood" today can be more than simply nostal-gic, it can raise "theoretical problems" for contemporary poetry. For example, in spite of all our knowledge (very paradoxically in this "age of knowledge") we live and have our being in a strange atmosphere . . . – for us creation is finished and dead, in it there is no continuing manifestation of the creative force, but the anonymous "laws of the universe," as if "given" once and for all – everything is geared to the world's being experienced as finished (once again, I am speaking here not of knowledge, but of the *perception of the world*) – what room is there for poetry to "soar" here? – and yet, I tell myself, I haven't lost everything if with my one-time child-self I can recall that once some-thing reached me that was more distant than the light embodied merely in the sun which stood above the village.

I have also my "personal" reason for returning to my childhood in thought-and-poetry. Even the human world that I saw *then*, connected as it is with those distant impressions, was nobler than what I have met with since. I don't think this is just idealization. It was a world of truly patient people, people of "village and field," their greatest beauty being the basic work needed for today and tomorrow – I lived in a world where the human imagination (and this is perhaps the very thing of whose creation it is said that it was made "in His own image"), yes, I lived in a world where the *people's imagination* seemed to be directed to its true destination; it was not bitter or destructive, but creative, "like God's."

*What is your general impression of contemporary Russian and world poetry?*

Frankly, my impression is that "something is rotten in the state of Denmark."

It is as if the Word has become rotten through and through, and not merely in the space surrounding me. Some kind of kernel has gone rotten in it.

The Latin word *religio* carries within it the notion of a "connection" – the connection of person, thought, and word with something Greater than the person. The word may contain this "connection"; – that may sound grandiloquent, but let us trust Dostoevsky, who says: "Everything in the world lives through its secret contact with other worlds" – you can believe someone like Dostoevsky.

In the contemporary word – or more exactly, in the action of this word – the connection I have referred to seems to be impossible. This connection is not a decorative piece of speculative moralizing or some kind of verbal "angelism." Shakespeare's Mercutio, when he speaks of the worms that will soon be eating his body, curses the Universe itself, its apophatic Soul . . . – there you have *worms-as-religio*! – these worms embody the "connection," becoming *words-as-religio*.

Clearly we should give some thought occasionally to ways of revitalizing the kernel, the root of this connection that lies hidden in the Word – "good intentions in the end lead to good results," as the French thinker Pierre Leconte de Nouy liked to repeat.

Forgive me for not saying anything about the outstanding achievements of the great contemporary poets whose word has the meaningfulness for which I am currently (so to speak) "fighting." I am speaking here about the general state of poetry, "among us" and "among other people" (in so far as I am familiar with more "distant" poetry). My general impression, my main impression of contemporary poetry today is as if its vocation was to *curse the world*, the world that in the end – with or without qualifications – we must call "creation."

Some thirteen years ago I was taught a good lesson by one particular creature – a starling in the Moscow suburbs. It was a dank day, wet spring snow was falling, the world was like a "curse." Suddenly I heard singing and saw a starling whistling away in the snow-and-rain on the steps of its little house. "What's got into it?" – it was quivering, and its throat was bubbling away. "It must be bursting with gratitude – even for a day like this."

That starling was much more grateful for its world than many of us who with rare zeal curse the day, the world, and ourselves as well – and even more zealously, our "fellows."

*What do you think about your intonations and punctuation?*

It's hard for me to describe my own intonations; all I can do is make a few comments.

I once listened to an old tape recording of a reading of mine as if I were listening to someone else, to something "alien." I was neither satisfied nor dissatisfied – "it is the way it is." In my reading I noticed several accumulations of psychological "waves" – I fear they broke explosively without the benefit of "self-control."

The first person to write about a certain "liturgical" character in my intonations was the Czech scholar Zdeněk Mathauser in 1968. From my point of view, I can say that the result was what I wanted.

I think my intonations contain something of the "rural-popular" sonority of *lamentation* . . . – sometimes I hear in my verse some clearly *feminine* intonations – evidently this is connected to the memory of my mother – "ultimately," I wrote in a letter three years ago, "what is called the people was simply the sufferings of my mother in such a life as had in her time been turned into something opposed to life."

I can speak more confidently about my punctuation.

Nearly thirty years ago I was extremely impressed by Nietzsche's words about "the supposed wholeness, not made by hands, of the work of art." The thought of the wholeness (even "supposed") of a single poem taken by itself became a persistent idea for me, and it connects with my punctuation, which is intended to eliminate the inevitable "seams" and "gaps" in a single, unified work – to replace them with elements of a "poetics of punctuation" which would be fully as important as the poetics of the "verbal texture." I admit that I am not always successful in this aim and that my punctuation is often highly complex.

There is a passage in Schumann about Chopin's punctuation that I have found very instructive. He writes: "In Chopin there are many secondary episodes and 'parentheses' which you should pass over on first reading so as not to lose the main thread. A composer does not like to disharmonize (so to speak), and yet we find in his music rhythms and tonalities notated with ten or more different signs that we all use only exceptionally. Often he is justified, but there are other cases where he complicates things without sufficient reason and frightens away a considerable portion of the public who don't want (as they see it) to be constantly confused and constrained."

My composer friends assure me that my punctuation is perfectly comprehensible to them and doesn't interfere with the reception of the poetry. But that is by the way. It's hard for the reader of a poem to be at one and the same time the "performer" and the "listener," and I am trying increasingly to reduce the number of "parentheses," to simplify the various signs that "notate" my verse, all the things "that we all use only exceptionally."

*Do you experience fear in the face of language?*

In poetry I do not experience any fear in the face of language (one should not "hesitate" before the "river" of language, wondering about the temperature "there," one should simply "plunge in," and there, as they say, "things will work out").

But I do feel fear in the face of language as the word of Prose (although for a long time now I have perhaps been thinking more about prose than poetry; in general I regard "great prose" as the highest form of verbal art).

I console myself with the thought that for me "the poet" and "the writer" are as different as for example "the painter" and "the writer," and that there is no need for the painter to be a "writer."

In a word, I am well aware that I am a "*non-writer*," and I only feel free in the "sphere" of poetry.

*Who are your favorite poets?*

I will name the poets whom I need just now.

Suddenly, reaching the age of fifty, it turns out that the two Russian poets who have remained most necessary and closest to me are Lermontov and Innokenty Annensky.

There is less "art play" in Lermontov than in any other Russian lyric poet. In a general way, he is not interested in "being a writer." Everything he wrote is penetrated by an agonizing central axis — I should call it the *axis of testing* of the truth that for brevity we can define in our time as *existential*. And Annensky, in my opinion, could be called the first "existential" poet in the history of European poetry.

In recent years (especially when I have had difficulty working) I have often read through the poems of Pierre-Jean Jouve. What I like in his poetry is the "dirt," visited here and there by "spirit" and as it were sanctified by it – I think this is like the "turbid damp" which gives life, almost "vegetatively" . . . this is the best kind of "action" in poetry.

*What are you working on at the moment?*

I always work on short poems only (I doubt if I shall ever write a long poem or a dramatic or prose work), and I am constantly working, since even the endurance of *periods of silence* is also work (and possibly even more necessary for me than "periods of talking": *periods of silence* seem to "forge the soul" in a very clear and memorable way).

It is worth noting that work on the word when *it will not submit* pleases me by virtue of a special quality: at times like this you may discover certain "properties" of the word, knowledge of which will prove useful in periods of successful work that remains almost "unnoticed" and sometimes even unremembered.

*What of communication in your poetry?*

For over twenty years I had fewer than a dozen readers (I am not thinking of those who knew my poems in translation – I did not know what they thought of my poetry). Evidently I can say that I learned to converse with myself. This does not mean that the other "I" who listened to me in one way or another was indulgent to me.

I do not know whether I am "hermetic." But I think "hermeticism" is a kind of respect for the reader ("if you want, you can understand this as well as I do – I believe in you, I trust you").

I have never spent time thinking about whether people understood me or not. Even some of my close friends kept telling me over the years that my poems were "absolute gibberish" (I can sincerely say that this never offended me). It is not true that my poems circulated in "samizdat" – apart from five or six people, no one ever copied them out by hand or typewriter ("samizdat" was only for poems with an "oppositional" flavor).

Briefly, then, I can say that I was not interested in the question of the "communicativeness" of poetry – how could I have worked if I had been thinking about this?

Even so, I must say that one type of "communicativeness" was familiar to me – sometimes I "come across it" even now. The poems that may be called "the best" are written in a state where in the process of writing you seem to be plugged into some kind of indefinable, undemonstrable "participation" . . . – all that is "best" in us is transformed into "creative" concentration, but perhaps it also encounters some kind of "creating force" which (I am convinced) exists in some way or other in the world . . . – for instance, I know from long experience that some kind of "connection" can be made between us and the trees in a forest, but we seem to be *swallowed* into the *essence* of these trees – somewhere "there," indefinitely "there" – as into a colorless darkness – the trees are without the Word, and we are swallowed into that *absence* . . . – but it may happen that in the light of Day something is *breathed* into us – we only know about this because within us, clearly and "in words," something – suddenly – answers this *breathing*.

We can say of a poem that comes into being in such a situation that in it "communication" has already occurred, although in such an "unconcrete" manner – the "consistency" of the poem is already made good by the imprint of the "communication" I have described. At times we can clearly feel its fresh trace.

*In your opinion, what does it mean to be a poet today?*

Clearly this is related to the particular nature of the time – in poetry I am very little interested in the personality of the writer. What matters more, it seems to me, is whether he or she "gives" me something of the world, the world of nature, the "universe." Spiritually, no one is poorer than me-as-"poet," but many people in the bustle of "action"-in-the-world (and these "actions" are becoming more and more monstrous) sometimes have difficulty in remembering that the "universe-world" always contains something that recalls to us not only the comprehensibility of life, but also its infinitely deep meaningfulness – this world sometimes touches us with bare fragments of the "miracle" itself – in its very essence, and this happens simply, as if someone were laying a hand on our shoulder, but this simplicity is the most inexplicable of all the things which we regard as existing.

To be "on the watch" for such gifts of the world, not to allow them to pass by unreceived, to pass them on to others in a "poetic" manner – all this, in my opinion, is the obligation of the poet today toward those who are interested in poetry.

# FIELD - RUSSIA

## PART ONE

# FIELD-RUSSIA

so this I wish you!
(happiness-prayer unspoken)
in the field to fall silent in soul ("oh God" we say
with more-heart: a valley
of white-gleaming
freely
all around
Perfection) oh how this wind
did not touch even radiance of breath!
fire
of unchangingness
wafted
the perceptible
all
was vanishing: oh then let it be
there
for a long time now
not knowing – as whom it was smiling:
"best Purest – you"

*1980*

# IN THE MIST

full of mist
all night the allotment – like a garden
and beyond it
beyond the fence in mist-forest
the voice of the cuckoo
as if in ever-quieter-unquietness
in the distant father-people
long
and long ago
my father
(in the crowd – billowing
with procession-and-singing)

*1980*

# WILLOWS

such willows: to fall asleep! be surrounded
with living silver like a sigh
and shudder and recognize the leaves in the shining of lines like
   a whisper (again – raised up by the sun)
of soft mist-caring – like tears in the world of silvery-shining
passionless childhood! – such willows: to fall asleep!
greyly to be scattered in quicksilver over tops and spill down
   tenderness: the one not known
the one painted in Spirit
and misted in death

*1979*

## FIELD: AND BEYOND IT
## A RUINED CHURCH

but this was long ago
and – thanks be to God! –
there is no other

and it seems
s o m e  happiness
(of *this*
place
maybe)
starts to ache with ("purest") pain:

oh in this state
("unto tears")
of gratitude! –

and in quietness (as if spirit stumbled
not understanding – and at peace with
not-understanding) – oh in this! –

in just such shining:

birches
are glistening
(as if
in this
the most Meaningful was happening) –

and it breathes – no-saying-where – oh it breathes
everywhere breathing! –

(and in the shimmer
so much more
the surfaces of the hill-circle seem miracles) –

and shadows
with quiet
speech of "somebody"
retaining
(like the soul)
their fullness
(both-giving-and-uninvaded)

shadow the field

*1980*

# SLEEP-ILLUMINATION

*to N. Ch.*

yet how many times! . . .
always whitening
(as with soul)
you torment
(but of sleep
such purity!)
– and how youthful then can I be?
such
(like a saintly woman's)
shining of torture-unforgiveness!
(and all – is not air
only – light)
– loving – you are doubled: in whiteness of fire!
(still with the same:
as in flight! –
burningly-steadfast *forsaking*)

*1980*

# AGAIN – FIELD-RUSSIA

As if – after vision of the air-sky-icon: of-the-Holy-Mother-of-God:
free it remained – goldsoftened by spirit of the people – the shining: of
Peace.

*1980*

# PHLOX (AND: ABOUT A CHANGE)

at times – we think: love
(yet there is only silence):
seems a single circle – of light – and quietness
for no one – since long ago:
already – with us – distant!
so now all summer already
(and more than till autumn)
you – as if unseen – you: in open whiteness
in shining unconcerned!
and living such a life (if I remember it as action)
looking as if blindly
I know (as I feel the hurts of children)
that yes: a little:
in my passing: playing – of life
you – like a certain circle
(from distances as if distance):
like a weak "god" in the mind (and therefore henceforth
already in free "eternity") – are lovely

*1979*

# AFTER THE BLIZZARDS

I with quietness at evening
(soul as if in snowdrifts)
know this: you are in the Land
and so – the breadth in the snows
and the shadow among them is such
(soul like repose of the field)
as looking into eyes we say "miraculous"
and sliding over itself
(and even more quietly)
as in open happiness

*1979*

# FIELD: SUDDENLY – A POPPY

in pale dawnlight
as if – before orthodoxy!
among petals
with hidden grains – "for no one" – this tenderest of cases!
(and it seems to be tapping
this weak orphan-like dawn
as if made of grief) oh wordless unhurried Greater
than offering of the "ready"! – oh quiet abiding
of the so silently Fulfilled

*1980*

# SLEEP-WHITENESS

*to B. A.*

"now
we don't often see one another"
(or rather:
don't see one another at all)
but – with a whiteness! –

secretly wafting:

(oh this coldness
mountain-top seeming! intense!
of the voice – as if white
with the best of treasures
*of the cypress casket*) –

but – with a whiteness! –

of a deep swooning:

with a fragrance: my friend! – I suffer
in sleep – that is lit: by your soul?
and – I do not understand

*1980*

---

*of the cypress casket*: *The Cypress Casket* is a collection of poems by Symbolist poet
Innokenty Annensky (1856-1909).

# GOUACHE

A field, littered with newspapers; the wind stirs them (no end no limit). I wander all day, I peer at them: the name is always the same (and the same forgetting: I have forgotten and I peer – time passes: no remembering); with always the same portrait (and again – forgetting). Where am I? Where can I return to? Evening; no road; rustle of paper; the Earth is made up of this field; darkness; solitude.

*1979*

# FIELD: UNKNOWN FLOWER

*to my son Artem*

oh luminator (oh for such shining
may I be forgiven)
oh lightreceiving luminator!
in the field toward matins-the-sun
with light-of-beauty
as with speech
of wisdom
shining

*1980*

# DISTANT DRAWING

*to the memory of Vladimir Pyatnitsky*

1

to see trees – is like sleeping
barely opening to distance
the edge of shining (and again – the edge):
oh this wind – after wind!
from "nothing is needed" and from "no one is needed"
(and ever more bright more bright:
"oh simply nothing")

2

to see trees is to sleep
unseeing to reside
having passed not to know it
to become less and less a light
and only melt in sleep in leaves
and not expect a thing

*1979*

# AGAIN – WILLOWS

*to my mother's memory*

suddenly
I understand *I remember your soul*
observing in mist far away
slopes now or islands or steps of the silver summits
of a willow grove
peaceful
(and in some way
"from beyond")
and "something" what is it
("magnificence"? "fragrance"
of intimate soul of "purity unspoken"?)
I must be remembering (and even far off in place of the face
I seem to retain in my thoughts
the quietest of hollows – now swirling only with tenderness)
and besides
this is only the flicker of "something" from memory
when the crossings
of *beauties* "not of this place"
cluster in that youthfulness
where the "eternal" is like orphanhood
(the unseen – awaiting our coming)

*1980*

# FIELD - RUSSIA – III

oh subtler than sky
lighting up Earth! – with people's soul
as with circle-of-love
"still more than lumen" burning

*1980*

# BUT THAT HILLSIDE

*to the memory of V. M.*

to incline the head
my melancholy hillside!
and hair in the wind
as by dark into air: always far and far off – falling!
in the wind to the grave
(soul just solitary – soul!)
and in shifting – a whisper (with remains of sobbing)
with wormwood – as with reality
(as if palpably-in-crumbs)
of the one and only in the world
(as if – here: the soul! – and a hand – as if into water!)
and of very-much-mine
damp solitude

*1980*

# AND: THE FIELD OF THE LIVING

field – like "something" like Appearance?
and if it was simply – for us?
as if "we were not" – only wandering in vision or deed
as if we were like advances:
strange – as sleep: in illumination!
we sleep we wake (as if we were fleeting):
we are for no morning!
the fiery light without meaning is empty
(only residual reflection without link – as if among us – not
    touching: the Gleam! – of the Fathers' spirit)
"meetings" "comings-together" – in empty-bright aimlessness
as if of a wandering (by light of day – as in unbounded unseeingness)
dream – of clods-of-fields as of clods-of-thoughts
in sharpness – in deadness – ascending! there is no awakening
in the Sleep-as-it-turns-out-Country!
in senile-childish (backward-turned) w o r d l e s s n e s s

*1980*

# ROSE AT THE THRESHOLD ALONE

but so much!
(all – of whiteness):

now soft shade a swoon
in the face it is shaking
the back of the head and thereafter
carrying off somewhere (as if into the purity
of all-disappearance) –

now with the return
(as if through a field) –

into whitest of white: itself:
more freshly (from long ago) shining

*1979*

# DAY-WORLD

Day – expanding – ever more – equality with the World:

>  as if
>  in movement
>  Coming-in of Words
>  and their Exaltation
>  in Multiple
>  diffusion:

>  (for
>  Emanations
>  seem a swaying
>  of masts) –

>  in a single Field
>  as in common-transparent-Soul! –

of Suns – in quietness – with cleanness of no-sound – the March:

>  into legs into back:
>  with Huge-Hours! –

>  once again building you.

*1979*

# VIEW WITH TREES

Night. Courtyard. I touch the birds on the branches – and they don't fly away. Strange shapes. And something human – in the wordless comprehensibility.

Among the white shapes – such living and complete observation: as if my whole life was seen by a single soul – from the dark trees.

*1979*

# LATE NUT-TREE

but – a nut-tree? nut-tree by your
patches
of rust
shall I be – or imagine? – a little
(when my "condition"
because of this
is damp)
orphanhood's wind! like a sign – to no one! – such a nut-tree you are!
somewhere – only as in hiding – including by chance
(myself)
for nothing
as if in the mist of a thicket
reflection of "peasanthood" without illumination
without things illuminated
of a kind of "life" remaining
in the wind
in the rain
to no one

*1980*

# DAY: I-ALONE
## (TWO POSTCARDS IN VERSE)

1

there where is abiding of the edge
of the poppy petal the tremble in the air
there – is the soul's attention: touched
by beauty "itself" (and a little
it seems with a scratch)

2

and blessedness of grateful contemplation
by the precious path of air:
glimmer of a bright-white butterfly
from heartsease to chamomile

*1980*

# OUTSIDE THE DOOR

but you must have – fear

so that yes: without a break
so that subtly: yes: the soul (for this we are as we are) –

and with life – also – that (and in essence it seems – of blood:

in aching – unceasingly – abolition! –

through oneself – through it – knowing:

and this – is all that is)

there was – a "time" and many times it was
now without any "times"
to have – such a fear
to have it – as if final:

(so as – to be alive
so as to be)

– but yet there was a time (that "time" is not)
when we knew-something-and-remained

outside the door – as if: the hour
(So as to take apart the look the cry)

a flicker: shadow-like – in the head:
as in the world: of unquiet rosecolor

(and besides – stillness: like eyes)
as if the Only-Spirit (three or four steps)

(So as to end – here: taking apart)

and a step – not a sound: like fur

*1979*

# AND: THE MORNING-STAR
## (BREAKS DURING WORK)

*to Csaba Tabajdi*

but toward autumn – ever more often: like a child
(when in sleep – it seems light)
with soul-wing unseen
(with a tinge of clear – with adulthood – orphanhood):
we do not think: "what?" but seem to surround
with a gleam the exclamations:
"but purity you are there"
(oh childlikeness is so long!)
then so much – is not! (like all that we are)
and after we are in minds
and again – weightier than all
(fallen
from the storm
of the World)
and all then
uninterruptedly
in sleep is like distant light

*1980*

# FIELD-RUSSIA: A FAREWELL

*Soon this too became known.*

D. P.

but to love the *motherland* – is not to see *Me*
came the sudden words
and the *country's* damp – in hollows –
heartfelt weeping: gathered life –

in the breast mistily grew – as once before – the space
where *proofs* of the Trinity swirled –

(as these
stars'
rising
you endured: as you grew – by Sleep!) –

words came in the night (and there is no word – without the Word):

only so much orphanhood: a mist – like a handful! –

to be eyelight swarming-oakwood-song
and to weep as a sun (because – without soul) –

and to be – a field – who is or is not – free

*1980*

# SONG FOR MYSELF

secret song: "I want for nothing"
and other than this
nothing I know
only that field too where in memory the soul is suddenly so simple
   and still
and the place too is such:
nothing there is ("I want for nothing")
just in boundless expanse the loose board of some building
in some way  s o  the person-somewhere-here
in some way an answering-song – to such daytime and lucid grief
like a wound in the hand but you look
and there is no looking away (and it seems this only remains
as some business and life)

*1979*

# FIELD - RUSSIA

## PART TWO

# FIELD: ROAD

with breathing (oh let me)
trouble it a little!
hide-and-seek of preciousness:
I shall say: for sleep I save it!
I shall say: I love: is it not with gold of shadow
of the sacred-in-my-dream
wafted and smoothed! such – love! –
to leave – even by light
(for a while I was: I know!)
but it is help to oblivion! and
you are more than continuation!
far off (like the world) – with unheardness
delicately – as from summits
(for childhood) of clouds:
to forget That which was audible
(and I close it – with a glance)

*1981*

# COMING INTO BEING OF A TEMPLE

oh
sky blue
and
field – in a silver thread – field
(and masses
of gold
masses)
along it – the tension!
and
with firmness of brightness
skyward

*1981*

# RYE – ALWAYS THE SAME – RYE

sun in rye – like my dream – as in scarlet – antique! –

quivering-and-slowly:

through tops of corn-ears (the way is lost)
my-life-sleep-oh-flowering-oh-Lord
moves in redness and cuts as with achingness-me
the dream – now vivid – of birches: here and there with nightingales
    (as if in places
in the wind they were hiding – not many
of a tender: in freedom: mind) –

it-grows-cold-it-touches as if in flight with nods-as-of-wafting-of-
    blood
the timid – through souls somewhere – places of nature –

somewhere in them for a long time (though we do not hear –
    but with gladness)
concealing heights of singing
(as if in their own depths)

*1981*

# OAKWOOD AND (ACROSS THE FIELD) OAKWOOD

*to N. V. Lossky*

1

eyes free among topmost leaves of the oakwood
I am a world without a brother
(and you)
but finding-through-air?
(I say
through the land)

2

but
continuation
in wind
(in touching)
noisily-with-children – you are now such quietness
with bones in yourself
of the fathers
enough for me through pain
to continue
as if into legs
into depth
eyes free among topmost leaves of the oakwood
for a long time now not going toward love
simply loving
everywhere where I am (and since then in awakenings
I was not set apart
to search)

3

oh writing into wind (more and more without pain)
become the people alone be the people
I would say to the friend (I shall find him)
the dawn is ever greater antiquity (it seems that we ask
of stars only) and peacefully
from blood
all warm
a brother rose up for me once
and for long
was continuation
in the people
(again
he will be raised:
not there
where it is not)
– always he is poor and always
sleep stretches wider than the world: so freely alive! –
I shall bring
so speaking
into clear air a roughness
"brother" – to be alive
to be – for a brother
(and this – let him be in his place)


4

eyes free among topmost leaves of the oakwood
a friend
(a brother but absences to me are indifferent)
in the bone (without weeping) is burning
(and for me
enough pain

"I" that "am")
and long I have known man's purity
for not with sight only
but with spirit he forged
(like a pail
full of water)
the ingoing (and trembling)
into steadfast brightness
of birches

*1981*

# SHUDDER OF A DAISY

little cloud! –

would once the moment
(invisibility-visibility)
of my death thus be shaken –

(what then
shall I choose
more dear):

wind – jewel-like – fleeting! –

as in flight
awakened in me – first of all:

freshness! –

of absence of memory

*1981*

# ROAD OUT OF THE FOREST

I am at home on the earth
I need nothing
but would like one small thing:
live suffering! –

(suddenly I see: the immense people only
explodes-gives – to-one-to-another
the heat of suffering: so burn with it apart
but pain is like a gift – of the family:

and in this we are neighbor food and brother! –

but that
freshness
called the people –

like your blood
hand
and breast
does not abandon and lives-enlivens:

sparks-reverberates explosion-and-fusion
and the small – in torment is great!
you will explode and color
the festival-singing! –

for they even offended
as if they gave bread –

for they even took away
the sobbing
as if
keeping
in cries too
the harmony! –

so – they tore the souls
so – kept them from deadness) –

– it will not be brother: here other festivities
will kill off the devil with this tedium
to be embodied (oh Lord)
in murderers – and in satan
himself – it must be! –

so *I thought* (as Norwid would say
at the end: I remember:
"*Vade-mecum*")
so I thought – coming out of the forest
ever lighter
(lighter than happiness of grasses) –

suddenly I see: through young oaks
gold is flaming
of-wheat-and-field – with a church:

(then
make room
for empty space):

and not a thing for nothing!
I do not know my grief
but the wind too is needed!
and in heat of gold my brother
no neighbor no little one
and so burns for-himself-"farewell"
that there is not any thought

1981

## SECOND LITTLE SONG FOR MYSELF

hair is shaken loose water poured
and for what – amidst this – the call
(so all presence of all also passes)
as of always the same – one and only – cuckoo?
(light of sleep is distorted – by shoulders once young
but still before the face it circles)
there so simple is grieving for love
– that has been a little alone:
of youthful light a-source-for-dreams-somewhere
is ever more sad and quiet – but the freshness already is – many
    times – such:
it will be late (all this is for the good
but only – such sorrowful good
it is not for you to speak of it)

1981

# FIELD-CONCLUSION
## (LAND WITHOUT PEOPLE)

In nature – d e s e r t e d (but "something" here whispers – in a distant "breath": as yet Not-abandoned) – we-I-or-something (there are now no "others"): we are – the r e f u s e r s.

Self-refusal-and-More (they went away – into heavens-without-mind – and the splendor dried up! – festivities of steel: in roots-as-in-crosses! – and it was – as in Heaven: in the Land-Dessication – from light as from wind! – we remember no "seconds").

And – mirage of a specter – false-height! – "here-and-there" this still is: *somewhere* this glimpse (without seed-center – without place: to grow into) but a rocking – a scattering! – to be the d e f e a t e d of those lit-as-by-whistling.

But "heaven"-from-a-thing? – with a streambed of emptiness: like absence – of wordlikeness.

There is – only blood (like movement of false-brotherhoods).

They came out of their age – out of echo-of-spirit-as-if-for-"eternity" (let us say so much) – fell out – fell into: the world's agelessness! – will not grow into infants: becoming – through this – the fathers.

And: there is (it creeps up mechanically-stickily) no People. The dying man will add (for no understandings): "who is the Father." (Soon will be no lesser word either – as of root-of-vision: for multitudes).

Field – without a word like "you" corresponding – field (like the Book) – with people: without people (the Illuminated-Eye – name-as-of-

Friend – and Second Sun! – cannot be broadened by us! . . . – already –
like dews – we shall forget it).

But – the o n e  w h o  s p e a k s?

(Yes. T h i s  also is  f r o m  t h e r e: *nothing has happened*, – and it
means one thing only: t o  v a n i s h).

*1981*

# APPROACHES TO SUNFLOWERS

I am lit – and at home
and forget all things
and again I am – with my brothers
to me – only light (and I do not know things in detail)
again – smiles
long since in-itself-receiving
pouring out with thankfulness
from circles-glimmerings-fathers
and only one thing I remember: as if shinings were shining
in echoing openings-touching
of sonority of breathing of feminine-sacrificial powers:
so all-embracing – like a world – from all sides
to me – a son also – whispering! –
thus you are the most womanly women (to the world of earth –
   more precious – than angels)
– essence of illumination! – with this-itself
for us – severed-brothers-in-the-Motherland
so were lit shelters-walls!...... and the gold of tears finished gleaming:
in air-the-whole-land-nostalgia
we seek – and the breath breaks out:
diminishing life: from shoulders!
(as if I by the whole human-shining
into dryness – of all minds! – above earth
were weakly directed – to shimmer:
in the house of shining
of autumn sunflowers)

*1981*

# FIELD (AND AGAIN – AN ABANDONED CHURCH)

Now:

what shall I call it? (perhaps – to the Soul:

of the once-Beloved:

a Memorial).

Visible: even a little (like breathing) – yes: in beauty (from within itself).

And – the rye: in continuing reflection (better be silent: from the fathers aching-as-in-bone – minds not reddened: we grow quiet).

(From time to time: blood-as-bearer: simply advances – making one who walks:

somewhere – without memory).

Anew.

(There is
the incredible
last word
"is.")

And – the rye (and no saying: "our own"):

it seems
the Original Field.

(But here
with voice
of singing already):

I was: let me be allowed:

(for the place – is for that):

as if to-speak-to-address! –

is there
is there not
something
but still
we know
the idea "but still":

with a breath
(as if coexistent with soul):

(quietly-resembling the sound of greeting of those so long already
    silent in circles expanding):

with a breath – like abandoned splendor:

to the place
(continuing white
with its
former whiteness) –

ever more distant (with spirit-or-ductility):

Purity-Rye! . . .

*1981*

# THIRD LITTLE SONG FOR MYSELF

but at times when for me it is impossible
(and yet possible)
"but there are such things for me" I then speak
my head: as if with it I dipped
in the motherland-somewhere-abandoned-distance
remembering "barely further but there"
oh how lovingly they let go! to weep with the cheek
forget I was loving
long against this splintered
this (now no one there)
field signpost – with the head
that had thought over everything – already stopped thinking
(no more would I need but now and long since and now not to be
    late
into this absence toward the tree-body
so that older alone)

*1981*

# PEACEFULLY: FIRES OF
# SUNFLOWERS

*in memory of Valery Lamach*

All around – a little – as if building: a house (I did not know – there I am: as my some kind of "many").

>    Again – let there be such a sunset (here too are things
>    of the fathers – still the same: to shift them
>    is my task – in peaceful motion-wandering).

I come into the light (but in the book on the table – words burn – and to me he was saying: "you are always giving" – but of that day – we could read in common brother blood: "explosion of joy in lightness of shining").

Only one friend was strangely-greater than the requiem (years were passing – he created: and one day the land – in his face I saw: in full! – did I worthily absorb that gold? – I dream of the face! – purity of circling – deserving or not – I know).

(Of childhood he spoke – suddenly remembered: the many disks! – and the book of books – and the many disks! – the freshness.)

And with this: "alone" – not true! – the gift – like August: and do-you-think-as-you-walk? in old gold: as in a chamber – ever more peaceful.

Have I forgotten? – to be gold with the fathers – suddenly: hands of my brother! – and of circle-fields – on behalf of my friend – unfailing: sonority.

(I wafted pain – saying that "with-spirit-ductility"! – he would have understood soundlessly – with the whole face.)

And brightness: as if building a house – for the people! – and yet my brother: for the spirits of few (a little is all! – when the face is fulfillment).

(I knew such a house of the people: as if I was touching the – communal – singing),

To slip perhaps – in grief (and memory is quiet: already the building of foundations is done).

> Ever more
> in softness – for no one – the sunset:
> and the striving of gold
> toward simple things of the people
> (but "they were" – means: they were).

Remembrances? not so: it is broader (as in deadness of the land – not from inside the land: a light).

And my friend! – brother: with a smile – as out of dear ones (I know – how to speak in purity of the face: from the face itself – and a freshness: brightness of disks! – light of sunflowers – like a house).

*1981*

# WILLOWS (IN MEMORY OF MUSIC)

*to V. S.*

in the long mist-vision
of bright inaudibility
through pain so clear and distant
is my holy duty – preciousness
of memory: to be sung – by beauty itself:
"schubert" as "mother"!
(you will not say "God" – oh God something
has happened to my soul: there is
no steady sobbing! and long now in somnolence
in such-not-mine-beauty
losing pure groans-summits
dimly I grow hazy)

*1981*

# FIELD AND ANNA

in the last
(how long then he continues)
bright – for the eyes of few – fire-twisted-as-in-blood
(image of the land of Ryazan)
the last one
is burning
(always I see
the iron of work
and the back
as in a bonfire
surrounded
by shouts
like another tongue too)
the last
long-ago-human
is flaming
(and already
my seeing
is not to be blinded):
what is it and for whom – this center-fate? – in the sun is less shining
    than in the neck or cheeks of burnt-out sufferings – in dimness
    longer than all fire! but the ancient
field
of Ryazan? it is dead
the field
and where now is
unforgettable Anna
dear-love-Alekseevna
where then are all your silences-passions? – and possibly a certain
    light not of the sun – whiteness whiter than snowdrifts of Russia
still glows and is charred

by your long-gone whispers that are needed
by no one in this field? . . . – we in such glory
did not open ourselves! – astonishments there were – just silence
of flame-ruin – in a circle-like-a-field
of burning fear! . . . – and deadness
ripened – of fire! . . . – and immensity was shut in the oneness of
    forgetting:
with no wind-manifestation – empty
Field – of fields

*1981*

## WALKING TOWARD A BIRCH-TREE
## IN A FIELD

it was
a – a
no more: it was
gleaming from within
(making clear the limits)
in soundless prayer
with movement – just barely
that heaven
too
should be
a

*1981*

# SLOWED AUGUST

the day was passing
as if with little leaves
with dear rubbish of Earth
in a world of rain (or a heaven of rain)
obscurely we were we swarmed
not catching fire not starting to shine – in the ocean
of god – like a boundless-white structure . . . – and it must be said:
this is quiet and hard
to live-have-a-being and not lift your eyes
so as to start shining – and like some material
in god (I shall allow myself this feeble knowledge)
to be dipped – being his own
downward – gravitation

*1981*

# MOTHER AMONG RASPBERRIES

and you were gathering
raspberries! so that I should remember (and weep) you
so that after a day after some quarter of a century
freshness like an angel (still the same one: movement
there was none)
was still coming in! beyond the river the voices
long seemed to be play-of-a-friend!
   now returned by the powers-and-winds of the world
in sorrow I am – through shadow: and besides
the mist is light . . . – friend do I really
know maidenly shining? (I disturb you
as if your light was for birth!)
spirit – for: tears! – this is sun of the clearing! – mist – a continuation
refining the woods with its ripples!
knowing – we know no foresight:
is god clear – and is it not better together
not to want to make him out? and only
to be – as if weeping with shining-friends
and with the self-motion
of berries long ago before sunset
in redness – to fall?

*1981*

# FIELD AND ANNA – II

theeeeeEEEEEEEeeeeere:

faʌʌaee:

(of a cry)

*1981*

# AND – A MEMORY: CLEARING
## IN SHAURI FOREST

but this one! and no approach:
with a disk – of light! with precision
of its bright closure! no repetition-plurality:
all – homogeneous! like breathing-firmness – with a gleam
suddenly – of Spirit – peering out: in clear absence of place!

(was it
with shine-and-circle
one time
at the foundation
femininity's sobbing?
rejected
by the land:
no remembering) –

further on – day breaks:

I was – space-love – of the family! –

and now: what? – (whisper or say goodbye: I must!) –

what? with purity perhaps of death-final-slipping
as if to breathe-and-pass-through
in flight – with gratitude-to-Earth
(here it shone too with Eye-and-Bone) –

in light that is lightless – above this to soar:

in a new – unheard-of – love? . . .

*1981*

# BRIEF APPEARANCE OF LIUDOCHKA

Meadow.

(To remember. To remember.)

Little-girl-butterfly.

Church.

Little-girl-butterfly.

Meadow.

*1981*

# AND: SCHUBERT

pain
for you
kept coming: in intervals of sky
in the young oakwood! how clearly
that blue might resound with your soul!
"music" they were telling me
I heard it – without sound:
it was my quietness!
later I learned – behind it
shines in longing such music:
as if – in reply – was made clear
in torment: our Lord! – and the one
we prayed for in grief – for us
in His pain grows quiet

*1981*

## POEM-TITLE: WHITE BUTTERFLY FLYING OVER A CUT FIELD

*1981*

## A., WALKING TO THE HERD –
## ACROSS THE FIELD

and behind his back
far off
a fullness
of shadows – with breaks – still fresh:

– with bright-damp whiteness! –

to the left – not rain but rare descent
here and there of clouds in the form of rain –

(and the lake of a gaze through the world
that one: now it cannot be scattered
and it turned out: sustained to the end:
understood: this is needful and true
when it is – for no one) –

– to cross the field? at times – across life: the passage through life! –

(but the one and the other:
pity
for some boy as if to a reed:
was there singing in the world?
no recalling –

yes: it turned out: the absence of singing-as-sharpness
was needful too
and somehow it happened:
this loss had ripened: and a whisper
by some thing-like-a-piece-of-clothing
was borne into the wind:

it turned out
this too was achieved:
as if they were asking:
and true) –

in the lake of the gaze is one movement only (although not
  remembered)
it may be
(since all can be)
through some kind of distant blueness
wind – as a sister! –

to the right – steadfast happening: a haystack

*1981*

# MIDNIGHT: RADIO JAMMING:
# UNKNOWN WOMAN SINGING

a voice
like weeping
*chenstokhovska madonna*
oh God:

"*Yanek*" (explodes)

(in a shout) "*Vishnevski*":

(unto-bleeding): "*is dead!*" –

it beats – on the Deadness-Land! –

a voice!
(now
nothing
is possible)
explode
if only
*a drop*:

there is such a one then
in some deep place
of peoplelikeness:

"*we can do no more!*" –

a voice!
plunge yourself

in the Century's making:
*"all is useless!"* –

soar up – in a final blow! if only at what remains
of the likeness of a heart
if only the one! –

*"Yanek"* (explode):

*"is dead"* (shout of Auschwitz)! –

cut (now useless but still cut):

into this Coffin-Land – into this "immortality" of death –
  "over-place" of deathmasks:

into this poster-people! –

splash out: *a drop* – alien bloody:

at "god" – or – at the wind-halo: over the Carrion-Place! . . . –

at the sky-conflagration

*1981*

---

This poem refers to Andrzej Wajda's film *Man of Marble*. The Polish word *pad'l* (is dead) suggests the Russian word *padal'* (carrion). The *Chenstokhovska* (commonly spelled *Czestochowa*) *Madonna* is a celebrated 14th-century Polish religious painting.

# FADING OF AUGUST

somewhere in the oakwood
made of sounds
a swing as if shining
secretly composing
holding back – in a state
of intermittence: all golden! –

a bird's: unknowing: farewell

*1981*

# ONE MORE LITTLE SONG
## FOR MYSELF

I am sleeping this is somewhere
this place where I am has long been without a country
but a consolation – somewhere logs under snow
the blizzard since then
and I too am not needed
friendship now – sleeves in ice
sleep-my-blood thaws on the tree:
how singing breaks out! with its shadow swinging
through pain as in all
in longing for posts-in-this-world-or-Gannushkins
in needless song rocking
in the field in the blizzard amidst snowflake-beings
with a forehead split open
singing into the world! – for the Lord
sorting through
the logs
under snow

*1982*

---

*Gannushkins*: psychiatric hospitals in Moscow.

# FIELD - RUSSIA

PART THREE

# CLOUDS

it was
as if
in God was the head
but remaining alone then
and it became clear: Day was darkening (there was work to be done)
and was shining – as it opened!
what was happening was consciousness – no doubt
it was melting with smallness-me
in That – which was opening the clouds like gates
forcing the mind – to shine! – and the frontiers
were time: were the breaks
in the vividly-single
(touching the Earth)

*1982*

# AND: MOMENTS-IN-BIRCHES

in the face
to grow heavy
and cut
with the part that pulls
as if into trustfulness of kin close by – into heavy and moist adoration
of brightness (as of brain) of birches
with a part
to cut
and in-clots-in-dampness
there from here
in tears as in bones in adoration
into whiteness-God! into deeper than a groan
with blood as with some blow
to fall! – in exceeding oneself to give (with that moist part
of weeping – as with fallings of firmness)
collapsing to give – somehow-splinters
to a Bow to the earth

*1982*

# TO AN ICON OF THE MOTHER
## OF GOD

in dreamings and visionings
in dawn day of nonevening
in the house blazing as with coals
benedissolution
of joygrieving!
in a corner-sanctuary that as with heart's coals
in dreamings and visionings
as if in the field the Living
at the deserted feast-table
like signs the many assembled

*1981*

# ROAD THROUGH A CLEARING

for fellow-feeling
with wind of the mind – so lightly drawn?
such a road then: so to hide it! – and then with grief
barely shade it! – and hold it back
just as far – as shadow in the mind! – but also shine through –
the idea of a smile: so that it is noticed –
in sunlight-sharp shuddering
(spilling over the edge)
in a grove of birches

*1982*

# DROPS ON A ROSE

but – drops?
is heartfulness (in good tears
for life)
still alive in children for me? – and in it
and even across it
these slidings? – and is vaporous tenderness
childishness fresh in the world
peacefully – dripped?

un-focussing (there – just as here):

segments dear – as in the house:

of this lightness-world! –

and little is needed of memory even:

I was – as I wandered from reading
(but somewhere
in damp they were young
and in visitings of the whitely-peaceful
I remembered: they are young! and over my face
that seemed distantly-weightless
for a long time – together
they slid)

*1982*

# THROUGH THE WINDOW –
## A CLEARING

weakness I would say . . . – is sacred
because
more than "there": it is like agreement – to be Beauty
of the unrevealed! just a little
here to swim up with it
out of distance and evening light – a certain
Selflikeness! – so to retain
(*Myself was as I was not*)
powerlessness of a weak and damp surrounding
living in flashes of light! – with a secret hint
of Visitedness – in grasses and branches . . . – especially
in saddening rubbish (*here*
*I touched on more – preparing for Myself*
*the strength to depart*)

*1982*

# UNTITLED

simply because it is so pitiful
I still call it love:
poverty, oh You-Mine! and the worst (oh, . . . I!)
so poor that in fearful nothingness
it cannot be – oh God-Mine! – unlove

*1982*

# REMEMBRANCE IN A CLEARING

singing:
in the beautiful – such little
steps: no catching him – oh Schubert!
he so: in creation of the beautiful-small
being (by virtue of the same)
the spacious-beautiful
(the Spirit Itself?)
slips away

*1982*

# CONTINUATION

but life's darkness floods the soul with likenesses
glimmer of sacrifice grows somewhere ever fainter
and time is needed: for the soul again
to shudder – having gone

perhaps in memory places of past sufferings
in a new order come to life again
and labor is continued: pains will cleanse you
of that same – sacrifice

and see – it seems that until now it struggles
transfiguring torment (all in blood)
and childhood chastity and maidenhood
in you – will start to weep

*1982*

# CORNFIELD – BEFORE RIPENING

gleaming
splashing assuagement:
                    discoloring
already – with oblivion!
and see: for now – it just clutches the spirit
for now – not purity (you remember heartfalls):

oh slowing! –

out of this ever subtler the seeing
and again the torment
outwearing the likeness!
and soon
soon – Bearing Away

*1982*

# FUNERAL OF POPPIES

*to A. L.*

so it was! – I buried the dream
and with it went the precious fadedness:
and without what netochka-nezvanova
is there windlessness now:

without the lovely "just a little"? –

little I remember – but in the world's Much
there trembles (is it not about you
distant person)

just a little disturbing: the message?

*1982*

---

*netochka-nezvanova*: Netochka Nezvanova ("nameless nobody") is the orphan hero-
ine of Dostoevsky's unfinished novel of the same name.

# EVENING THOUGHTS AMONG
# RASPBERRY CANES

*to Léon and Simone*

breath of happiness
when from out of raspberries
it turns your head! . . . –

guessing:

what was that – beatitude? –

home?
(to be sure: this was in the family
and in childhood – with loved ones
all around) –

it was homeland
(and only including
the forgotten home)! . . . –

further – friend – destruction (and calling it "life"
they continued it for us
and we too) –

but – it remained (and the head is turned
by happiness-as-distant-memory)! . . . –

so – at evening among the canes
we searched for berries
of the forest (with peaceful blows
in memory of much seeing):

what brings back – with a jolt of radiance
home and country? and family (with illumination
of the host – of those loving in kinship)? –

what – at last – from a letter – from raspberries – of forest and field
from a home-like-stone
can bring us the breath – of beatitude? –

(oh this freshness: we touched
the thing itself – with illumination-steadfastness
more steadfast
maybe
than the concept-world) –

this – is she who loves like home (with a spring of
    illumination-childhood) –

and continues: with kinsfolk and country
and our destiny
still incomplete! . . . –

in the breath of raspberries I know
where the radiance starts: like breathing I see
a child's – a woman's – face – somewhere:

simply – I should say (I lead to a simple conclusion)
I am glad of happiness
for happiness that is! –

a wonder – this is always simple (but a mystery – it is simple – but a
    wonder . . .)

*1982*

101

# PARTING WITH A CHURCH

what more do I remember? –

now – just windows ever emptier
(ever more – wind not wind
gleam of light not light):

as if they – were e s t a b l i s h e r s
o f   t h i s  that there should be no  l i n k
with this space abandoned! –

and Silence comes in like a warning:

communally-one – into country-and-field (and ever more whole – in
  desolation):

:

as if – the  o n e - a n d - o n l y  Church

*1982*

# DREAM-IN-A-BANNER

time
of Throwing
of Haystacks! – and you?
as if I am spreading and just the same I-peered-in:
still the same on the haystack
work of hands of torment of white clothing:
vision-you – like a banner!
I burn-and-am-seen both by you and myself
and in purity of impulse against you-all-widespreadness
the same golden wind is troubling you
ever more long-gone youthful-burning!
and in him – the untouched movements of love
are exchanged and the gleam
into distance – soaring

*1982*

# OH MY FRIEND

can he
be dead – the guardian
angel? and deathly – appear
as the bearer of Words? – for the phrase is strangely-distant:

"soon you will come . . ." –

and is whispered – by a friend
who is quietly-deathly-calm:

all is motionlessness!
and only the cause of presence
like – muddied waters . . . –

as if – yet a while: is it some sort of "time" or is it
displacement? . . . – there would be a light –
insubstantial . . .

*1982*

# REMEMBRANCE IN A CLEARING – II

The White.
The Black.
Stone – is both one and the other.
Poor houses:
Arles.
The Black.
The White.
Shade – like invisible ice. In the middle:
fire
(eating away
the more-than-Poor).
The White.
The Black.
Field – unfathomably gleaming
(in hugeness of the world)
invisible
ice.

*1982*

---

*Arles*: city in southern France where Van Gogh lived and painted in 1888-89.

# LATE LAST FLOWERING OF
# THE WILD ROSE

the soul remembers it seems about blows
and purified – radiates
sanctifying wounds it preserves for itself:

all – besprinkled! –

oh this air – of unpeopledness! . . . –

(he has died
it seems
whom I cannot remember:

and to wander! – to nobody then
as if guilty – one word)

*1981*

# SOLITARY SUNFLOWER

*to V. Sokol*

oh tremble of solicitude!
(better not
lift up my eyes) –

surrounding myself "I-a-child"
with a modest surplus of joy
in myself – at playing – myself:

– oh you my person-poem!
(more tenderly
I cannot say it) –

(but here:
I say: but here:
visibly:
the secret:
of the golden: section:

and here I cannot even whisper) –

oh be:
what you are:
as completion!
(but modesty
is like the flow of a tear!):
– permit me:
alleging:
it is – in the One:

to abide – and not name it in words:

with circle-you – to see in Spirit:

oh perfection! – to perfect

*1982*

# AND THAT NUT-TREE LONG AGO

*again – to my mother's memory*

but the cold
the clarity of cold?
that the place should be – in quietness
still clearer: "but the soul?" – in coolness!
and – in the wind: a child!
still the same: hands in dampness
on a dear cheek it seems:
but now – just attainment in beggarly shuddering
of windlessness – as of absolute-ice!
with just glimmers of cold
back to one's thinking (as if something had
emptied from meaning) and to jointly-silent clothing
as in falling aimlessly returning
with relics of movement:
of that – for it happened: *whom*
*shall I tell?* – when since long ago
*any* places – to me
are only – as if made of absences!
(and in such:
unconnected:
of people's ice-"feeling"
oh still mother-touch)

*1981*

# ISLAND OF DAISIES
# IN A CLEARING

*to the outstanding percussionist Mark Pekarsky*

illumination
moving (............................................) –

! –

aaaaÁAAÁaaaá
(voices and voices and voices):

:

– ⓘ – ⓘ – ⓘ –

illumination upward (voices-and-glimmer-and-voices):

:

..................................(oh radiance-drumroll):

:

*1982*

110

# DREAMS – WITH FACES OF OLD

and both in snows
they flowered and in roses
summer long they sought out
encounters in me with islands of white
and spring waters
oh God of such being! – as if the soul knew
their sources in the world – and tested them
in forbidden communion! as if in the ancient image
not restraining itself! the soul all: returning: in signs
as from sacrifices! . . . – from snows and from roses
too innocent (and even through love
there is no communion: as if remaining
through singing of the church
without song!) –

. . . "life" they called it all life they called it! but then – others
   whispered . . . –

and I
through idea-like-snows-through-snows
can see – them otherwise wandering: by shining
(if only from pains
in the remnant!):

what then! – under guard-as-with-signs-of-torment:

(already
without shelter
in disasters):

*roses! – in-blood-through-snows-and-in-suffocation-you-roses*

*1982*

## ONLY THE POSSIBILITY OF
## A FRAGMENT

... but this Gold and Heat
is a relic (as if the Sun "was")
of the Meaning-Appearance "*Rye Ripens*"
like a Roar without Place
like Collapse ...

*1982*


## ALWAYS THAT SAME WILLOW

a cloud of old
as with movements of thinking
there – in the very same stirrings –
as if amplifying a nearby-damp sensation of the face
closes for me
the place of ma-má-veneration as in babyhood
so that I can endure
and not holding me back
it is utterly silver

*1981*

# PHLOXES – AFTER "EVERYTHING"

*in memory of Paul Celan*

but Whitene-ess? . . . –

(t h e r e  i s  n o  m e) –

but Whi-iteness . . .

*1982*

# THREE NOTES FOR AN EPILOGUE

1

but tears
no longer nourish what we call "bodies"
changing with the clean
but also with our faces
we were long delayed: already there is no
becoming – in illumination! and if we are shadows
then – already through feeble increase
of false-belonging to daylight-just-empty
in the Land of No-People! and is there
a little – *for something* – of grief? – if only
in this drop! . . . – but with it
the place you will not even mark
where Absence only is lit! unique in this
*"to the pure all things are pure"*

2

"But tears, – they change the outward form of the human face."

3

but each one
each-one-individual – is within a fire!
so much fire: so much emptiness-without-everything
(removed too the meaning of seeing
and the basis
in roundness of heaven to recognize the face that is no less close in
    sympathy
than the nearby-neighbor-face)
each one (or better – no one) – is within the empty and dead

fire for him (and there is fire enough) –
seeing
the face
of no one
(even the blade-of-grass-image)
and the tree-(oh-whisper!)-face

*1982*

# PURER THAN MEANING

oh
Transparency! just once
Come in
and Spread yourself

in a poem

*1982*

# CLEARING TOWARD EVENING

but
it came about: the clearing
is wholly change: already – advancement
of light – to that fullness: radiance
all around – of peace! – and only the surplus
somewhere above – in vanishing delicacy:
as if – seen by someone! – but the look
removed: and to us remains
only the sensation: of pure
(all-giving)
departedness

*1982*

# TIME OF RAVINES

# ROSE OF SILENCE

*to B. Schnaiderman*

but the heart
now
is either mere absence
in such emptiness – as if in waiting
the place of prayer
had grown quiet
(pure – abiding – in the pure)
or – by starts pain beginning
to be there (as perhaps
a child – feels pain)
weak nakedly-alive
like the helplessness
of a bird

*1983*

# YOU-AND-FOREST

I was hiding you burying you then
in forest illumination
as if building a nest out of you
(I did not know that both fingers and birds were playing
and coming into being
for a music unknown to me:
timidly-supple to pulse in air-clots of trembling
so – to touch: as if not to touch)
I unwept I forgot how that forest was coiled in a hearth made of love!
visibly unknowing continues without me
I have become
credulous
toward emptiness
and so for me the age is already new!
"I need nothing" and suddenly you illuminate
from the youthful ancientness of the fathers
and unexpectedly – ageing – I am shattered
in golden rain: oh alien vision! – perhaps your chastity
is to be – without it:
continuing ever the same: in the burning of people-fathers – in an
   already distant inaccessible refuge:
in this steadfast blazing – in endless snows
in the dampness of work – as in rains – continuing-to-temper-the-
   Allpeople
you remain unknowing – in what reverse circle
they burn – my imaginings-visions: at such a distance where even
   their semblances
burned out long ago! . . . – and you
like my brain in youth: shining image in clear light of day:
are struck and are twisted
from the fullness of those same depths

by a pure – like your hands – like the idea of them in this world:
light – like a whisper! . . . – and simply – perhaps
now this is all – only through me rustling
the name – of the people

*1982*

# WITH SINGING: TOWARD AN ENDING

*to A. Nazerenko*

*The festival had dispersed. I saw only a small line of
people going off toward the forest.* (Noted in 1956)

with the sway of the forest's hem
the line departed – smiles among them – vanished
taking with them the singing also
step by step departed with the sway of work with hands
leaving me for a little while
the flutter of the forest's edge:

– no nothing will explode I shall be stifled in calm:

oh god how calm is my God
to fall silent so openly! –

simply with such simple
covers of light of clay concealing blood:

to flash into the forest – finish sparkling as in heat haze
in that it only remains to me in a single lightbone
dimly to appear in faces:

that give birth to earth! – for heaven:

(here I must forget and of poor things be silent more poorly: this
power like things unneeded is too weak even to die: it is wind
rustling long since in destructions – even blood is not needed:
to be spilled as a sign – and such a waste place – an indifferent
eye! – and it will be earth more and more – for day):

and so it is time to awake
for more than the God of stillness:

for the phantom of light it is time to awake
for the light of absence of brows — unveiling us
with peals of fire:

what then? we shall sing to the end: expect nothing
so again to awake as to water
"oh line" to the walking-line:

– God take at least such a thing as living

oh it must wake (and the forest closes):

in quiet weakness the weeping-line! –

you – who have not finished singing

*1983*

# ABOUT A LITTLE GIRL AND
# SOMETHING ELSE

evening
but the roses
of human misfortune are not immense that is why the name also is
   too flat
"mommy has gone" she says as if asking
for a drink – "where to?" – she repeats "she has gone" (there are toys
  and there is this simple idea)
this sudden little girl (simply – there's no one to return) – and on
   comes
(as if years and more years were passing)
a windless evening – oh roses
here injuries too are as if they were not – but still
someone keeps coming to the window and playing the fiddle
as if we deserved
to be busy with withdrawal
here among the ravines – and roses I would like just a little
but now there is nothing little
so as to remain with something simple – and playing the fiddle
in a strangely-open way he keeps coming
to step back from the window
as if without shadow: and seems to know injuries greater
to lend without loss! . . . . . . – and not forgetting
the evening windless
as the little girl's simple understanding
with no meaning-details: is simple

*1983*

# PITIFUL LANDSCAPE BY AN UNKNOWN ARTIST

*to I. M.*

tall dry stems
of grass: thus unending – and out of the Sun
seems to pour – a passionless word from the lips
of a wise man of old: *but pale: it visibly:*
*finds it hard to mock* . . . and with brilliant noise
the world is no longer expressed: what it utters stumbles
like a broken stalk . . . other . . . continued
to the edge of the earth . . . – but the artist clearly gave up
seemed to sigh . . . – and in this grey haze
(barely perceptibly) suddenly shuddered
two or three daisies

*1983*

# THE LAST RAVINE
## ( PAUL   CELAN )

*to M. Broda*

I climb;
thus in walking
one builds
a temple.
Breath of fraternity, – we are in this cloud:
I (with a word unknown to me
as it not in my mind) and wormwood (unquietly bitter
alongside me thrusting
this word upon me),
oh, once more
wormwood.
Clay,
sister.
And, of meanings, the one that was needless and central,
here (in these clods of the murdered)
seems a name to no purpose. With it
I am stained as I climb
in simple – like fire – illumination,
to be marked with a final mark
in place – of a summit; like
an empty (since all is already abandoned)
face: like a place of painlessness
it rises – above the wormwood
(...
*And*
*the form*
*was*

*not*
*seen*
. . .)
But the cloud:
they grew blinder (in hollow facelessness),
the depths – without movement; the light
as from openedness – of stone.
Ever higher
and higher.

*1983*

## LITTLE SONG FOR YOU AND ME

but this trouble of ours is a twopenny affair! not worth calling trouble
it does not walk – barely toddles
does not hammer on the door – rustles over the road
and is not a shadow – like an empty hollow in fire!
trouble only because though the grief is slight
as if close by – with some kind of a mark! . . . – and like some
    poor rags
(and very much alive) it is stirring
and again – like the semblance of a sigh!
so do not look around then:
since at just such a time it can say
more than God (but perhaps it has been said)
and after long waiting trembles

*1983*

# STREETS AND RAVINES

*to M. Fonfreide*

of islets
(all to me)
that summer consisted:
I say: flowers: and an islet and others
again – damp with tears – there
in the street
and somewhere beyond the ravine
and everyone – in soul passing by    was
(such visible rustling):
my living friend (supple glimpse of an embrace
from the image
again
will splash out
more than once)
it was – as if annensky was near
and like childhood a little girl coming to me in an apron:
it was that very radiance
trembling
close and dear to me! . . . – and in glances full of life
communication
gleamed
in my quietness:
I lived in landslips of white . . . – and by sleep
I was passing – like time

*1983*

# A DEAD ROSE AMONG PAPERS

On money
taken from the poor,
to fulminate – with sovereign powers.

Shall we call it shameless?
Even with this – to give them something.
A cause – for pleasure in others' woes.

But *something*, be it ever so little – to the *poor*.

But, oh my God, what are we speaking of?

Even the word *poverty* is not allowed us,
and that
it should be
on paper – simple.

Rather they will snatch bread from a child.

Out of his hands, a pitiful crust.

*1983*

# LITTLE SONG ABOUT A LOSS

*to Peter*

long
like a desert
in such freedom it starts:

further – still further – more fathomless seen
carpenters laying (reddening and ever more distant)
logs on the wooden foundation:

and they weep as they fall on a log –

but this is such boundlessness
in sleep-clarification-of-the-edge-of-burning:

so it was purified – no more will anything be:

and even – no seeing: with the soul! –

and only reddening (and ever more distant)
they weep – as they fall on the log

*1983*

# BEYOND THE TIME OF RAVINES

all by which I shall die about that am I now
in other things
continued: a ragged-ancient slippage:
and what is there to say:
and yet – fresher than the birth of leaves
in the midst of those islands (like children's souls laughing but
    without them) –

those islands – I say – of tufted grass
(as if in their midst
I in soul in a smile
was long since without myself) –

and it trembles among days
like the one and only Day:

abiding: the glimmer-of-love! . . . – only something a little – of a
    stranger's blood:

but such a thing – rustles: and one time you will wake – with this! –

and why repeat it?
this is a circle: with the Sun too not vanishing:

just as if
you agreed in the All-field to vanish! . . . – but the gift of the spirit:

divides what was divided by the clever-unwise:

in order – through and through! and by triumph – with no bond! –

to be: through abiding – untouched by the world:

(wind – above the ravine)

*1983*

## SCATTER OF PHLOXES
## IN THE OUTSKIRTS

but grief?
the possibility grows
of letting it go somewhere . . . of following:
and – freely – with its evident islets
this day grows unquiet! . . . –
– and in it now here now there are white landslips:
who speaks through them? air like fire
since long ago unseen-not-natural
only in fatal depths! I roam
with no greater aim than the birds:
in a game: that radiates emptiness: light
is drawn back – and
the places – like landslips – of people
are in flower without forms in fire like something pitiful
and – as if they were secrets: they drown! . . . from such
an outskirt I whisper – with lostness
in a little happiness (like light of ash
on paths: abolished: like thought
for me the ancientness of phloxes is stirring
and the life in their midst
and in them
at one time – with dear ones)
rather – I gaze
with the stirring
(than
in white
places
with thinking
I drown):
that long duration is now greater than life

and our abiding like the outskirt
swells with nonrecognition! names
will move away from meaning:
it is wind of the world
(now free
without flowing – of links:
it eats itself up – with exhaustedness!
and trash – is rustling)

*1983*

# UNTITLED

who – through silence
speaks of the equal dignity – of peace
in front of the Creator? – it is slowly-reddening
seconds – of wild roses
inclining a peaceful conjecture: we
also – might be included – but only with stillness
of the same – kind . . . – but  t h e r e  we drown only
in voids where meanings are never answers! . . . – and again to our
   own silence
we return
as to the truest word

*1983*

# AFTER MIDNIGHT – SNOW
## OUTSIDE THE WINDOW

grief
like orphanly scattered-white clothing
(as if
of a hidden event
the fresh
departure)
to begin
and widen
through a silent land
just – everywhere – breathing desolation
the field (oh grief) with some blank spaces
(as if all is finished)
of souls

*1983*

## ENTERING – A WOOD ONCE ABANDONED

I enter – in walking receiving: circles-glimmerings like a gift on
    myself
as if shining with an unseen river – expanding – just such a river –
    into myself – somewhere ever greater!
I am losing myself – do not seek – even more – I remember more
such then is the finding of peace – there was whispering about that
    oh there was
but now through luck for felicity there is not even this
only so continuing to be you will be ever more yourself –
    incomparably losing that faintly sorrowful "yourself"
and in going out quenched: it may be – out of my sleep! . . . – oh
    how long ago I was
and how much
ever more – you are – only you! – some kind of Soullikeness is stifled
    (as if I can still observe it)
and – in a flash letting through: suddenly – a landslip-of-light
and only the one – Began circling

*1983*

# AND: THE ONE-RAVINE

*to the memory of Krysztof Baczynski*

1

this tranquillity
wind over the ravine by-People-called-shamelessly-Ravine
and at last the Super-dignity-Abyss – and simply such a calm
collapse-Dignity: there is nothing it signifies Unity (to this degree
    to the moment
by talking to the end
wind
over the ravine)


2

wind
like breathing already with Nothing-and-No-one we say
spiritlikeness (likeness of a likeness)
of the Friend-depths-of-first-created-Auschwitz – of the all-human-
    Thinker-with-trenches
wind
dream not dreamed to the end
sensing (and the soul like blood from a baby with banners tearing-
    and-crying in wide-opening)
sensing-eating in endless dog-breathing
the crater of the ravine
the ravine
and only out of liquid-substance-"once-upon-a-time"
this inverse long-before-Someone (when already like a corpse over
    everything the name
had stopped shining! – the absence
of traces shines – beyond that end-of-shining)

oh this
inverse
no less
Rain

3

oh quietness
I was not more shameless
with you quietness
but now even so with me
you quietness are like breathing
of light-immortally-high
of the spirit-of-Ash (in such true
beauty
now
you are
quietness)

4

wind
we have finished but from the ravine
shamefully but still like a flower
the wind like the babble of baby-Baczynski (here for you is a flower-
    such-a-hieroglyph-of-super-perfection-trembling – and now it has
    arrived like the wound of the child in its subtlety shameless)
wind
over the ravine
they have finished
even brandings of perfection of shining to grasses and birds teeth-of-
    perfections-of-Humanity-of-god-long-ago-Selfeaters
and even some
sign

to the wind
through Emptiness itself
cannot be drilled home or sparked off
end-of-shining
has covered: and there is no name
of-what-or-of-whom-That-now-to-give-a-name-to-is-empty-and-
   late! – of that: in closed setting aside!)
only bones are shining not light of eyes over the face!) and a kind
   of endlessness
without-dots-and-dividing
of shamelessness in ultimate subtlety
tearing-Something-tearing – and more and more subtly! – they have
   finished – wind over the ravine
they have finished
wind
over the ravine

*1984*

---

*Krysztof Baczynski*: Polish poet (1921–1944), killed in the Warsaw Uprising.

# HILL-FOREVER

*to L. Putyakov*

hill
burning and melting the thoughts all around
how it was borne in on you
that distant poor-free childhood
of a friend in torn clothing: how this fire all-embracingly entered
the spaces between brief appearances:

(a child – was briefly passing) –

but from these open spaces I composed a tenderness
early-adolescent – clasping brotherly movements
shuddering possibly from the depths
with a gleam-of-people in all-people fire:

(no less he was – a friend) –

and in the venerated flame-ancient-hill
these silence-landslips (like airy clearings)
seemed church-shining-blue
from bits of childish clarity
cracking my collarbone
burning –

*– and since then there has been a long time so long as if absence of*
*thought and of world – circle long ago closed! –*

and not the hill burns but emptinesses
burning-answering the blows
of that earth that gapes (if only "in our home" but we all are already
ourselves)

and became end of sound – in conceptions-places also!
windlikeness only:

hollow echoes
with the idea of home-exhaustedness
with no – directions! –

but of impotence (since as forces we knew the weak and departed
    progenitors-welders of the heaven of love out of laboring clods
    – with simplicity of labor – and of clots of soul) –

the specters of power impersonal-faceless

can be seen
as thunder on thunder
landslip on landslip:

in one sky
of non-meanings – unique! –

. . . you cannot even say in what circling all this remains . . . –

(but the friend?
the true name
of any friend is – Loss:

and for me – "no matter" . . . – for me it was long just a snatch of
    old song:
it was – "a child was briefly passing" . . . –

but I know it: hill-forever)

*1984*

# PHLOXES – A GLIMPSE

once
in days such as these
Thou – wert:
(can it be? I am left with unknowing
but with strength – that is greater: since then
never changing):
it suddenly – flamed: with wounds – that stared
as if with a beating beauty-question
a kind of road-body – into the breast – from depth of noon
(a fragment! body-path – in collarbones – in the neck
and in wasteland of the outskirts):
did the flowering tremble: no-greater-love-possible?
more painful than life – the shock! thus – suddenly
it came in – it struck: like blood on blood?
and from beauty – I did not suffer but: "if only death"
(I wandered – no tear shone white: day
was scarlet – more desolate) now
I seek – as with the ghost of a tear: now? "oh what you will"
only – into *that* love! . . . (by chance – as if secretly
straying – among phloxes)

*1983*

# NOT REACHING THE PLACE
# WHERE A FRIEND IS

*to Jacques Roubaud*

this
is not wind
but through long freshness an evil
slippery-rosy – as if with whispering
of movement capable
feeling-of-disaster: this something – barely shudders
in the house – as in the field:
white
it stands
close – to books: as if shining through – by the bank
of the river where remains – a fragment of light: just some kind of
    gleams-and-shreds
of unhappiness – in grasses: and suddenly – at once – like open
    night: naked – into the dark
and illumination
in it quietness:
as if they kept on walking – in a circle of light
precisely and brightly . . . and again
in the warmth there is badness: and with crumpling of breathing
again – close to the face! – shifting direction
with something – still the same – rosily-formlessly swelling
in your house

*1983*

# LEAF-FALL AND SILENCE

1

so that I
in myself should pray,
You
are not filled for me – with prayer,
and in evident powerful
absence
I am ringed, encircled.

2

But in her
the child – I cannot
pray. She is in herself
a prayer. You, in this quiet circle
Yourself
are utterly
in Yourself.

3

What am I
in the Silence – as in steady Light?
Or in fire. But the sick trees' frozen equality is living. And You, next to
    this –
are clarity, – oh, impenetrable clarity. Compared to it
death is a promise . . . – is something other! . . . And in a dead circle
unendurably
falls from a tree – a leaf.

*1984*

# IN THE PEACE OF AUGUST

recovery:

between shoulderblade and neck
it lies hidden – as if like an unknown living substance
naïve and golden
human silence –

ripens for memory:

until now there was not a word – and now – like a breath comes in
the half-empty shining:

a still incomprehensible prayer

(as for a child)

*1984*

# ALONGSIDE THE FOREST

but
at last I draw near there is no one there never was
only silver
of ancient feeling – in free warmth over forehead and shoulders
oh
this weightless
field – in its shining to heaven

this
is soul of solitude like a glimmer of shyness
existing all around
and free it shines white by my side
but purity is brought forth – simply – through purity itself
the field
manifestly
(still just like
a field for heaven)
glows with it – to itself

what
of other things? the shining pierced through
in order – to love
as it were some angel – all around – my unimpededness
creating thus
the place of chastity:
– whatever winds there may be dark departures or lives
this is quieter than the god of quiet!
there
in the silence
blue

*1984*

# FINAL DEPARTURE

## (WALLENBERG IN BUDAPEST: 1988)

In 1988, when I was allowed abroad for the first time, I spent the summer in Budapest.

I had long been interested in the outstanding Hungarian sculptor Imre Varga – I had retained a particularly strong memory of a reproduction in a magazine of a sculpture of the poet-martyr Miklós Radnóti, a victim of Hitler's concentration camps, whom I had translated into Chuvash.

On one of the first days after my arrival, my Budapest friends took me to see the monument to Raoul Wallenberg that was designed by Varga and erected in May 1987. Thereafter, I often used to sit in the little park where the bronze Wallenberg stands, and all through the following month, not yet knowing what kind of poem it would be, I worked on a subject that would not leave me in peace, even during long and tiring journeys all over Hungary.

The initial title of what I was writing was "Wallenberg's Hand" – the strangely enigmatic, stationary, yet "moving" gesture of that hand kept finding its way into my rough drafts. A year later I began to look for an epigraph for the poem I had completed, and turned to religious literature. In theology the Hand is defined as "the instrument and sign of action, expression, communication." The levels of meaning turned out to cover an enormous range: from "power" and "possession" to "dismissal" and "consolation." All of this, as I remembered more and more clearly, was to be seen in Varga's remarkable work.

"Son of the Right Hand" was the name I privately gave to the great Swede (the expression is used for the chosen of the Lord, who is "Man"), but for the poem I chose a title and epigraph more appropriate to the silent, restrained, sacrificial attitude of Wallenberg.

Let me note finally that the words *Khaya* and *Aum* are taken from the refrains of Hebrew lullabies.

*January 1991*

1

this
is *no one here* . . . – but in fact: the long completed
common
and single
final departure –

like a world stopped short –

(and there remained – to the one remaining
the long
crumpled dampness
– somewhere on the neck on lapels on sleeves –
of the long
growing old of a host of eyes) –

this
is the frozen-in-trembling (insubstantial specter
of some eternity)
black-toothed mouth
of the simple thorn –

keeping far from the lonely – unchanging – hand:

at the very same distance –

(here

nearby
in the alley) –

this town of hawthorns – August
Eighty-Eight – and in its clear center
this single all-human
hand – this from long ago
is *just simple Simplicity*
of beggarly-plain-eternity: like
down-at-heel slippers
in Eternal Con-struct-ions
for
Gas Chambers and Hair . . . –

2

town of wild roses . . . – only this hand
never rests:
it is incarnate
in eternal Consolation
of the long-since consoled: it remains – oh: with
no one and nothing – the Consoling
most
lonely hand
in the world –

"here" – it has stopped – "here
is the door"
(to say more – would be
to displace
that same God: and thus
still more – to be

damp-boniness-fragility
in greater Abandonment): "here
is the (railway-truck)
door" – and the *simple*
slowly-eternal
*removal* – of the hand:

World
*With No one* –

:

(just a faint trembling

*K h a – a y – y a . . .*) –

3

and as if everlasting
like air like light –

this gleaming:

still the same
hand . . . –

long ago
parting long ago with the *Heaven of Wordlessness*
it unendingly falls to the pit
in be-ne-dic-tion of the terrible
Earth – like a S t o r e - H o u s e (oh how much of this
I know

as through Universe-Sleep) –

damp
with the steam of unseen blood –

(nearby the hills
lift themselves
in sweat – stirring
out of distant valleys – and with-tattered-rags-to-the-wind-only-
    praying
backs . . . – long since unmoving
silent as the hand – and now never
again will it tremble
the hand) –

– the trains have departed:

oh: *K h a y – y a . . . –*

*A – a – a u m . . . –*

and Time
*carrion-spectral –* has become
the minute
(oh at last) of farewell
long ago –

Long-Ago-Unending

:

(. . . t h e y   s i n g . . .) –

4

this
is the One Level
*Higher* – they have scattered speaking-and-singing
*Lower*
*They Keep Speaking to the Hand* (and shouting) – such is
the Trinity
in the blazing heat –

(for
*In the Middle is the Hand*) –

in the town of hawthorns (always gaping
*in those*
alleys-and-shouts
oh
black-mouthed) –

and – again
comes in the pitiful
childish *dance-likeness*
with no one:

*K h a – a y – y a –*

(not even a ghost of air)

oh: *A u m* . . . –

5

– a sudden blow to the face: for there was
another hand
white – on red balcony railings
beside the azaleas –

(suddenly it shuddered and vanished
and the world
became – a piercing nail in the forehead:

oh: this
first *center of fear* . . . –

– *and yet no one shouted out* "mother") . . . –

6

the silence of the hand
became a world – and soaked through cracked open
s t i l l   n o t   a b a n d o n i n g
it had long dismissed (such a hand
takes leave – *for itself alone*
never taking leave):

like God stopped short
(no other
will there be – no other
only
*His Stopping*) –

here

is this  p l a c e
of the hand . . . – and above it
the Gaze of the Lips:

so – as if in light flight
barely trembling they look
only – at children . . . –

(and
how afterward
mingled
with this childlike importunity
the crushed in-fir-mi-ty of ra-di-ance
of holy-beggarly-bystanding
lamented by somebody
bodies – yes indeed: as of *materials*
but still
e v e n  s o – the Lord's . . .) –


7

and the dreamed-of Timelikeness
ascending (Whither-Ascending)
long since – without movement: became
the last boundlessly-single
moment of Rescue (the *clang*:

. . . as if – piercing his finger . . . – with the needle
oh God! – Schubert's needle . . . – the *clang*):

the face darkening
becomes
a continuation
of the Final Door:

(oh how many there were: *fields* and *valleys*
all
from the *black*
*doors*) . . . –


:


oh: *K h a y a* . . . –


8

maybe
I am Dream without Self
where they sang laughed and wept
*straight away they were nowhere but they sing*
only the hand does not leave
its Level
above Earth: they went and will go
and it only remains: through branches
stare
clouds
(oh – dirty-toothed) –

– the trains have departed – the harmonica
alone to the whole Earth
sings
in the world
in a tattered hawthorn bush continuing
the rain and its solitude:

*K h a* – *a y* – *y a* . . .

*August 1988, Budapest*

# FOR A LONG TIME: INTO WHISPERINGS AND RUSTLINGS

Whisperings, rustlings. As if wind were penetrating into a cold store-room and flour scattering somewhere. Or – straw trembling in a yard abandoned by all. The rustling is the coming into being of some land.

"To be a mouse," said *that poet*. To be a mouse. Vertiginous. Ripples. Afterward they said it was poison. Half-a-Pole. Ha-alf . . . As if behind the whispering of clothes was a cut. From the slaughterhouse. And hidden in the rustling – blood. Even if it was only man-clothing. Alone, alone, – with the liquids of torture.

But reb-be, made of all things – of *this* and of *that* – you were so much one, – dirt, a torn book, and blood, – oh almost Transparency, – winter dance in the street, tattered jacket, man-snowdrifts (for everywhere was the sweat of poverty, – even in straw: there – in the wind, and the scattered handful of flour).

Life, rebbe.

And then, – here. This face . . . – all-embracing. It is as if you are walking through the city, and everywhere it is "mine," every corner of it. Vertiginous. Then – the ripples. And even if it was only: a garden (all this is face, in the face) splashed out there – inaccesssibly. It sprang back, pain – as from glass. And – *you cannot squeeze in.* "A garden – just a garden." Like a popular tune. Bottomless. And – close at hand.

And how does it happen in the voice – some bottom lies concealed. And do we converse in words? Wind. Bottomless. You cannot name it – even with signs.

And this man from Hungary. Simply – a fraternal grave, no more. They dug him out – *with all the others* (and this is what matters most) into the light of Day, and suddenly – there was the Motherland. The question solved. *With all the others* (this matters most).

"God" – not the right expression. There is only: "And God?" For ever and ever.

And then – those journeys. Rol-ling stone. For prizes. And speeches. All correct. In honor of. And all – seems: floating-in-air! And as if through heaven it wan-ders: pain-language, – alone, – for heaven. All empty. Give up the ghost, – huddle up, – only pain. Language? – the Wind of the Universe.

Oh how simple it is. This "simple," there is no place for it in language. (You can try. Straight out will come – a thing. "The simple," – such Freedom – compare it: the mind brought collapse.)

Ripples. Simple, vertiginous.

Oh, whisperings, my clothing. Straw. T-r-a-sh. Oh, rustling, my skin. I-motherland, I such-clothing-and-flesh. With whispering-skin.

Ripples.

But no one cries out. That-is. Not I then. "I" is sticky. There is something other (behind – the whispering. Behind this rustling).

And in the water walks the sight of this Frenchman. Car-r-ion. What is this, – the essence? – the clothing? The one-ness.

Forget. Oh, when then. Forget. And – p u r i t y  b e g i n s.

And.

Ripples. With all the dirt – of torture.

No floating back up.

No-*Baptême*.

No-o.

*1991*

---

*that poet*: The Polish poet Aleksander Wat (1900-67), who fell foul of the Soviet occupiers of Poland and was exiled to Kazakhstan during World War II; subsequently, like Celan, he emigrated to Paris.

*rebbe*: a Yiddish word for rabbi, master, teacher, or mentor.

*And this man from Hungary*: The Hungarian poet Miklós Radnóti (1909-44), a victim of the Holocaust; during a forced march with a large group of Hungarian Jews, he was shot and thrown into a mass grave.

# Afterword

Gennady Aygi is already known to English-speaking readers through a number of published volumes, notably the bilingual *Selected Poems 1954-1994* (Angel Books and Northwestern University Press, 1997), *Salute – to Singing* (Zephyr Books, 2002), and *Child-and-Rose* (New Directions, 2003). All of these contain information about the poet's life and writings, so I shall limit myself here to a brief biographical sketch followed by a few words on the poems that make up this volume.

Aygi was born on August 21, 1934, some 400 miles east of Moscow in a village in the Chuvash Republic, at that time part of the Soviet Union, now included in the Russian Federation. His first language was Chuvash (a Turkic language), and he eventually became the Chuvash national poet – besides writing originally in Chuvash, he translated much foreign poetry into his native tongue and assembled a remarkable anthology of Chuvash poetry that has been translated into several languages. But Aygi is above all a Russian poet, having switched to writing in Russian largely on the advice of Boris Pasternak, with whom he was friendly during his time at the Moscow Literary Institute and who remained a vital influence on his work and his vision of the world.

His friendship with Pasternak and his own unorthodox poetics combined to expose him to political harassment from his student years on. During the Soviet period he remained virtually unpublished in Russia or Chuvashia at a time when he was becoming widely known, translated, and admired abroad. He lived in Moscow and was married four times, having five sons and two daughters. In the 1960s he worked at the Mayakovsky Museum organizing art exhibitions; after being dismissed from this post, he made a precarious living through translation. His life was difficult, but he found support in an "underground" of like-minded creative artists. Only with the *perestroika* of the late 1980s did he begin to be officially published and to receive recognition in Russia and Chuvashia; at the same time, he began to travel all over the world, received many awards, and was several times nominated for a Nobel Prize. He died of cancer in Moscow on February 21, 2006, and received an official state funeral.

Aygi's essential work is a series of lyric "books" which taken together make up what he called his "life-book." Because of the difficulty of publishing his work in the Soviet Union, these books rarely appeared as separate publications. The present volume, which was planned by the author shortly before his death, contains complete translations of two of them, *Field-Russia* (*Pole-Rossiia*, written in 1979-82) and *Time of Ravines* (*Vremya Ovragov*, written in 1982-4), followed by *Final Departure* (*Poslednyi Ot'ezd*, written in 1989), a poem in eight parts devoted to the memory of the Swedish diplomat Raoul Wallenberg, and by a short tribute to Celan in poetic prose. These are preceded by a long interview given in 1985 that casts a vivid light on the way Aygi saw his poetic work at the time when these poems were written.

In Aygi's view, *Field-Russia* occupied a central position in his work. It was begun after a particularly tragic period in his life, dominated by the politically inspired murder in 1976 of his close friend, the poet and translator Konstantin Petrovich Bogatyrev. Aygi had overcome the immediate impact of this traumatic loss in what he called the "explosion" of the luminous lyrical work *Time of Gratitude*, which carries an epigraph attributed to Plato: "Night is the best time for believing in light." But after this explosion Aygi fell back into silence, and in January 1979 he wrote to me of a "fearful inner dumbness since last summer." At the same time, however, he declared that "gradually I have come to the firm knowledge and certainty that *I have had enough of despair.*" It took him many months to find his voice again, however. In January 1980 he wrote: "life – apart from day-to-day worries – is above all a difficult spiritual search for something to live by; previously everything found a voice in the 'poetic' word; now there have come to be some 'spheres' of life where there is no Word."

In 1980 Aygi spent the summer with his family in a Russian village – a stay that was to be repeated the following two summers. It is principally to this that we owe the new beginning that *Field-Russia* represents in his work. The Russian countryside, the villages with their ruined churches, and the people around him all spoke to Aygi of spiritual and moral values that were more and more retreating into an inaccessible past, and that he felt compelled to reassert. At the same time, the fields and woods of the Tula region recalled the treasured Chuvash countryside of his childhood, so that in writing about Russia he was also proclaiming what Chuvash and Russian rural cultures have in common. I can probably best shed light on this by quoting from a series of letters I received from him between 1980 and 1982.

On June 19, 1980, he wrote: "We have been in the country for five days now, 140 kilometers from Moscow, in the Tula region. Our village (with twenty houses) stands in a clearing in the middle of deep forest. All around there are oak trees, reminding me of my Chuvash childhood. I can't tell whether my Chuvash soul is weeping or rejoicing.

"And the hills, hill after hill, they have started speaking together in such a Russian voice (such an ancient Russian voice! as if there was something 'iconic' about them). I write – and with my shoulders I feel-and-know that the hawthorn is flowering now in the mist (the human soul cannot know such tranquil solitude; I am reading here the writings of Russian *holy men*; behind their sayings there *stands* their silence . . . – I jot down some verse – and despair . . .)

"But, yes, – I am working [. . .]

"All May I was very ill [. . .] and for the first time perhaps I discovered the beneficial effect of illness – I was feeling devastated and then suddenly I felt that some kind of 'meaningful' silence had entered this emptiness: I started writing in a 'new genre' of tranquillity and feebleness – something of this survives here too, in this unGodforsaken village."

On his return to Moscow in September, Aygi summed up the summer experience: "We spent two and a half months in the country; there was such a feeling of Russia coming to an end (and in the people it had already come to an end) – a state of more than grief, but at the same time of more than 'happiness.'" Six months later, on April 1, 1981, he was anticipating the coming summer: "A month or a month and a half from now, God willing, we shall be able to go to the country, and it seems a very short time since I was writing to you from there – from a blessed place, from 'Field-Russia'! (So life passes, and that is good! Although I am more and more glad to be alive – as no doubt a tree must feel in middle life, having got used to the 'usual' ups and downs of life.)"

On June 20, he wrote again, and the letter conveys well the contradictory feelings that run through the poems of *Field-Russia* (enchantment with the village and its surroundings, but at the same time grief at the disappearance of a precious world): "I am writing to you from the same village from which I wrote just a year ago. This time, I have a lot of work to do in the vegetable garden [. . .] It's a lot of work, and a lot of pleasure, the cucumbers and potatoes are already in flower [. . .]

"Here, among the marvel of the golden encircling hills and the incredible fields, it seemed last year that I was touched by 'the one who breathes everywhere.' I am quietly longing for the return of that 'breathing,' and continuing the cycle of poems I began last year, my most 'Russian' cycle [. . .] But it is hard to cast off the feeling of 'orphanhood' (relating to the land and the 'people') in these wide spaces that are so dear to me."

In the following year, Aygi was still writing poems for *Field-Russia* – many of the poems in the third section are dated 1982. But at the same time he was working toward a new book, *Time of Ravines*, as is indicated by this extract from a letter of February 3, 1982: "I began the year in the darkness of my own depressed state (brought on by bad news, directly concerning some close friends). But thank goodness I have taken a grip on myself and am writing some new things (in a rather muted manner) – possibly the start of a new book.

"'New,' that is, in relation to the book of poems I wrote last summer. Those were months of unusual emotion and exaltation. I should love you to see those poems – somewhere and somehow. This cycle undoubtedly contains an inward conversation with you (these are not mere words, you are one of the two or three friends with whom I inevitably and naturally carry on a kind of 'hidden' conversation, when I am free and alone in nature)."

*Time of Ravines* is a new book, then, written in a rather different manner, but there is much to link it thematically to *Field-Russia*, above all the desire to assert spiritual and natural values in the face of grief, oppression, and loss. It is also worth noting that the composition of these poems overlapped with the quite different cycle, the very joyful *Veronica's Book*, which was devoted to the first six months of his new daughter's life. *Time of Ravines* seems to me a more "Chuvash" book than its predecessor, principally perhaps because the "ravines" of the title, which figure in so many poems here, are a prominent feature of the Chuvash landscape. A significant feature too, for during the years of the Tatar occupation (from the thirteenth to the fifteenth centuries), the Chuvash peasants (who at this time lost much of their culture and their written language) took refuge from the invaders in the ravines that cut through their fields. In the introduction to his *An-*

*thology of Chuvash Poetry*, Aygi quotes from the composer Kheveder Pavlov: "Chuvash poetry was a 'song from the ravine,' because the working people, suffering from an oppressive yoke, did not dare to settle in open places [. . .] In Chuvash villages it was only at night that you could hear from the ravines the sad songs of girls celebrating some festival."

The modern equivalent of the Tatar yoke is only hinted at in this collection (radio jamming, psychiatric hospitals, Van Gogh at Arles, . . .), but it is always a dark and threatening presence. And there is open reference to one particular figure, the tragic German poet Paul Celan, whose writing was a cardinal point of reference for Aygi at this time. Celan appears as the posthumous dedicatee of one poem in *Field-Russia* and as the subject of "The Last Ravine" in *Time of Ravines*, where the image of the ravine seems to relate not only to Chuvash geography and history but to the modern landscape of the Holocaust.

Somewhat later, in 1991, Aygi was to write his tribute to Celan, *For a Long Time: Into Whisperings and Rustlings*, and it is not entirely a co-incidence that the same year saw the publication in Russia of *Final Departure*. Here the black history of World War II, which lies behind Celan's poetry, emerges as Aygi's principal theme. But here, too, he rejects despair, centering his poem on the heroic figure of Wallenberg, who was instrumental in rescuing thousands of Hungarian Jews from the Nazi extermination camps, only to perish himself as a prisoner in Soviet Russia.

Aygi also can be read as a "nature poet." Many of his poems take their title from natural objects: fields, clearings, hills, ravines, trees, flowers, snow, air. He is constantly alive to the world that surrounds us, above all the world of the Chuvash or Russian countryside. Nature is a sure source of value; like Wordsworth or Hopkins, Aygi sees in it an essential spiritual force that human beings need to preserve, respect, and love. To a certain extent, the natural world – the fields of

Russia, the ravines of Chuvashia – is a refuge from the losses, pains, and degradations of human history. Yet this human history, and in particular the tragic history of the twentieth century, is at the heart of Aygi's poetic enterprise. As I write this afterword shortly after the death of a poet who was also a dear friend, I hope that the reader of this volume will appreciate the truth of what Agyi said in an interview from the 1970s: "Poetry, as I see it, can do one thing only: preserve human warmth under the cold sky of the world."

*Peter France*
*Edinburgh, April 2006*

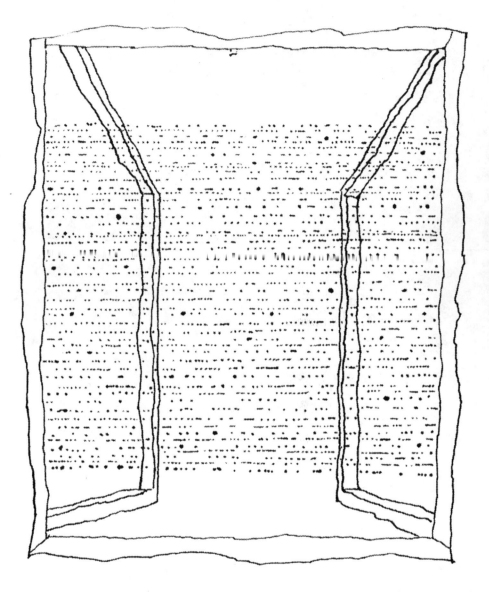

*Igor Vulokh*